Financial Planning for Managers

A. H. Taylor, MC, FCCA, has had varied experience in the financial and marketing areas of a wide range of industry and was secretary and chief accountant to the UK subsidiary of a major American corporation. He now combines a principal lectureship at a London business school with consultancy work.

R. E. Palmer, FCCA, was financial director of EMI's UK Records Company, and his earlier career was in private practice, the Ministry of Supply and the chemical industry. Mr Palmer died in 1977.

A. H. Taylor and
R. E. Palmer

Financial Planning for Managers

Revised edition

Pan Books London and Sydney

First published 1969 by Pan Books Limited,
Cavaye Place, London SW10 9PG
3rd printing (revised) 1975
Revised edition 1980

ISBN 0 330 26070 7
Set, printed and bound in Great Britain by
Cox & Wyman Ltd, Reading

Contents

Introduction

It is something of a truism that we are living in an era of planning and control. The causes certainly include two world wars, the development of international trade and competition, advances in technology and successive economic crises. Whether it be the housewife with her housekeeping allowance; the industrialist with his responsibilities to shareholders, employees and other interests; or the chancellor of the exchequer with the burden of his national budget – planning and control is part and parcel of our daily lives. We may not like it. We may even resent it when it is imposed. As an act of self-discipline, however, we have come to realize that it is an essential factor in national, business and private life.

The purpose of this book is to explain in language which businessmen can understand the nature of the assistance which the financial function can provide in the planning and control of a modern business. The authors believe that the needs of modern business make it essential for all managers to have a sound appreciation of the financial implications of their plans and actions. In this competitive world the key factors are costs, prices, turnover and profit; these are the factors which no manager can ignore. It is consequently no longer sufficient for monetary considerations to be regarded as the exclusive prerogative of the accountant. The accountant is essentially an expert adviser on financial matters in the same way that the engineer is the expert on technical matters, the personnel officer on human relations, and so on; but the manager must be conversant with all functions of business because it is he who makes the decisions.

It has been said that the objective of business is no longer profit but survival. It is equally true that no business can survive for long unless it makes an adequate profit, for otherwise the investors who supply the capital will take steps to wind it up and place their money elsewhere. Profit remains the overall measure of efficiency and the sign of success. The determination of profit is the ultimate aim of accounting exercises and it can be expressed only in the all-embracing medium of money. Thus money is the natural language of accounting although, as will appear later in this book, financial management also makes wide use of quantitative measurements other than money. In this sense accounting data reflect the result of an immense assortment of human efforts.

The scope and function of accounting

Accounting is a technique, a science and an art at the same time. It is not an exact science, however, like mathematics or physics; and like other forms of mental discipline it is in the process of change and development, a process not unmixed with vigorous but healthy controversy. In its basic and probably original form, accounting consists of the recording of transactions in a purposeful manner; that is, purposeful to the owners and managers of a business. The auditing function has developed side by side with the recording function, no doubt because of the fallibility of human skill, and indeed motives, in the presentation of financial information. There is evidence of auditors being appointed on behalf of both the state and the owners of capital from early days. In more recent years the internal auditor, acting on behalf of management, has grown in influence and moved towards the audit of systems, especially in the field of data processing.

The recording function remains the foundation of the accounting discipline and may be said to lie within the province of a skilled accounting technician; he will be served by a number of bookkeepers, who may be described as the craftsmen of the profession. The accounts kept by business are essentially records of the inflow and outflow of funds. Funds are obtained from investors who become part-owners or shareholders; from loans, such as those obtained from banks and from debenture holders; and from creditors who supply goods and services for which payment is deferred. The funds are applied to the acquisition of assets of a tangible nature, such as buildings, plant and materials, and those of an intangible nature, such as patents and good-will. Further values in the form of men's time and effort are purchased from the funds to produce added values represented by the stocks and services supplied to customers. When the added values have been sold a profit should arise for the owners, and a vital function of the management is to decide how much of this profit should be distributed to the owners in the form of cash payments (or 'dividends') and how much should be retained in the business for the purposes of growth and security.

Running alongside the basic records of assets and liabilities is the analysis of the extent to which the various operations have produced added values, and the extent to which the prices paid by the customers have given a surplus over these values. This analysis is presented in summary as a profit and loss account, further broken down, as required by management, into what is frequently a complex structure of operating accounts, sales analyses and costs.

Accounting looks into the future

Just as the prime function of the manager is to plan for the future so are the higher levels of accounting designed to aid the managers in the formulation and control of their plans. This is where accounting assumes the character of both a science and an art. It is scientific because the accountant's function is to evaluate the proposals of management by logical analysis based on the evidence available and to give precision to the comparison between alternatives. In the long run the plans of management are plans for alternative uses of capital, and their relative merits need assessing in terms of money. The imperfections of money as a measure of efficiency will be discussed later in this book but, as human society is constituted, it remains the final gauge of success or failure, at least so far as business is concerned.

The art of accounting lies in the fact that while the accountant is endeavouring to give precision to future plans, the facts and figures available to him for this purpose are inherently imprecise. Thus the costs which are likely to be incurred by a factory in carrying out its production programme will depend, amongst other factors, on many human qualities, such as the skill and motivation of labour and the efficiency of the management. The inflow of cash which will be generated by a sales programme will depend on external economic conditions, e.g. the intervention of a credit squeeze; and the prices paid for the goods and services involved will be influenced by seasonal changes and political trends at home and abroad. According to the needs of the management the accountant may be required to present projections showing the most optimistic, the most pessimistic or the most probable situation which will result from alternative applications of the business capital. In addition to the art of dealing with uncertainty, the accountant must adapt the picture which he is asked to present to the personalities of the individuals who are intended to read it.

The forward-looking aspect of accounting is usually called 'management accounting'. This is a title of somewhat recent invention, which some accountants regard as unfortunate for they maintain that accounting has never had any justification other than to aid management in one way or another. It does seem that the anxiety of recent years to treat management as a kind of academic pursuit has resulted in the creation of a spate of new descriptions of old-established techniques. What, it is suggested, has really constituted a major change is that the accountant is no longer able to practise his traditional mysteries in isolation from the remainder of the management team. His job is no longer confined to recording what has occurred, what is past and, therefore, irretrievable. He must work in close contact with managers responsible for research, buying, making and selling, and aid them in controlling the future. The only possible value of past records is that they may act as a guide and a spur to future planning.

Managers and financial planning

The range of learning required of a manager, according to the current spate of management literature, must be calculated to give even the most successful businessman a profound sense of inferiority. The number of sciences and disciplines which he is supposed to study in depth is perhaps only exceeded by the number of books on the subject. In this context the task of convincing managers who are expert in their own fields that they need a sound knowledge of financial matters is particularly difficult. It is especially difficult because the words 'finance' and 'accounting' have no aura of glamour about them; rather to many people they have a faintly sinister connotation. To some people the sight of a statement containing many figures produces a slight feeling of nausea. It is possible that this psychological antipathy to figures – especially those recording costs and values – has developed because they have been presented to managers by accountants and others as a record of failure and inadequacy. It does not help when the manager who is told that his costs are too high or his sales too low does not understand the conventions on which the figures were compiled and therefore considers them suspect.

The situation could be remedied in two ways. First, less time should be devoted to fruitless inquests on past performance which is history and beyond the possibility of remedy; second, managers should take a more active part in compiling the figure-work which gives light and precision to their own plans. The manager should be in a position to demand the information which *he* requires; he should use the figures as a means of simplifying his own task, of reducing the element of guesswork and chance in his own decisions. But if he is to command the situation in this manner it is reasonable to suggest that he must make himself familiar with the nature and purpose of financial management, of the principles and concepts of accounting, and of the major conventions and techniques involved. This does not necessitate an extended course of study; it is largely a question of being able to use the advice of the expert in the most effective manner. It is not even essential to have a knowledge of mathematics, although some skill with figures will help because of the logical processes of thought which are demanded for their manipulation.

One of the themes of this book is that there is nothing particularly abstruse or subtle about accounting or the financial measurement of forward plans. The trouble is that, in an endeavour to trace the sources of profit and loss to their ultimate beginnings, many accounting techniques have become so sophisticated as to lose their reality. This is particularly true of the detailed process of allocation and apportionment which is sometimes used to produce a figure called the 'product cost'. In some concerns the cost of a product or service is a compound of so many bits extracted from the expenses incurred by a business that it is not susceptible to analysis. No wonder the manager grows impatient when he is asked to control an unknown quantity of which many of the ingredients are beyond control!

The need for long-term planning

Frequently, the businessman is so immersed in day-to-day routine that he tends to be oblivious of the changes in external circumstances which are occurring around him. As a result, decisions based on action that was successful in the past are no longer valid. If it were at all practicable one would say that every decision needs a reassessment of the situation and a renewed process of objective thought about the problem. The changes which affect a business, whether it is a local shop or a major international group, are reflections of changes which are occurring on a national and international scale. Widening communications and the emergence of new nations are creating new markets with demands for new products or modifications to old products. Developments in technology are intensifying competition on an international scale by producing new materials, improved mechanical devices, and more efficient systems. Every business is affected by the growing complexity of government controls, largely of a financial and fiscal nature. Perhaps the most fundamental changes are those in the structure of society such as the emergence of a powerful teenage market, the increased power of organized labour (not always organized by trade unions), the growth of education, and certain changes in ethical standards.

Changes of the nature indicated above demand at the same time both flexibility of management and increasingly heavy investment by industry. They also clearly demand considerable qualities of forecasting and foresight. Flexibility is essential so that a business may be able to make rapid revisions of its plans as and when it appears that they are no longer suited to meet changes in external circumstances expected in the future. A business which intends to survive cannot afford to be producing goods and services to meet the demands of last year. Most of the factors of change involve investment by a business, that is, the spending of money now to produce income in the future – often the remote future. Investment is increasingly required in research and development, improved machinery, automation, the establishment of administrative and operating systems, and the training and education of personnel. The management dilemma is that the investment takes a long time to recover in the form of sales while the changes in external circumstances are often of a short-lived nature.

The rapidity and unpredictable nature of some external changes cause some managers to assert that they cannot see ahead further than six months or so. Nevertheless, unless a company plans for many years ahead it becomes merely a vehicle for opportunism, without purpose or stability, and likely to be too delicate to weather the winds of change when they come, as they assuredly will. The first responsibility of management is not merely forward planning but long-term forward planning. Because money is the one unavoidable limiting factor in business the conclusion is that financial planning must rest securely on the long-term intentions of the management team.

The foregoing, subject to only minor later amendments, was written by the joint authors as long ago as 1968. In the eventful years which have followed, many of the trends foreshadowed in this introduction have become accentuated if not fulfilled. The management of business has become an even more demanding occupation, requiring increasing knowledge and skill. Technology, especially in the field of electronics, has continued to develop rapidly and has been the cause as well as the consequence of more rigorous competition and expanding demand. To survive in these conditions, a producing business needs to pursue a policy of continuous technical innovation and this in turn involves a highly adaptable marketing function. Successful technical innovation can rarely be achieved without substantial investment, thus imparting a renewed emphasis to investment appraisal. Nevertheless, it remains true that, however brilliant the technical expertise and however effective the marketing skill, the survival of a business will ultimately depend on the margin between price and cost; the price must be acceptable in the market and the cost must be controlled.

The manager operating in this environment can no longer be content with the conventions and routines which may have been adequate in a less demanding era. There is a greater need than ever for flexibility in the day-to-day conduct of business; at the same time management must devote more effort and time to initiating and evaluating a continual flow of investments. For many of these investments the fruits will not emerge until perhaps many years in the future, and for most of them success is overshadowed by risk and uncertainty. The nature of modern business is likely to enforce a new dichotomy in the management structure: between the *administrators*, with the flexibility of mind to cope with continual change, and the *innovators*, with the vision to foresee and initiate change. This is not the old and somewhat academic distinction between the administrator and the planner; for the administrator, who is also a manager and not merely a technician, has always had the responsibility for planning his routines.

It must follow that an accounting service which aims to provide effective information for managers must also adapt to the changing demands of business. If the speculation at the end of the preceding paragraph has any merit, accounting must also adapt to the changing nature of management itself. The accountancy profession now has at its command, for the purpose of processing the data it uses, that modern slave of the lamp, the computer – with even greater but as yet unfulfilled potential in its progeny, the microprocessor. Nevertheless, the modern demand of accounting is not merely to churn out masses of data, much of which may be ignored and some may be irrelevant to the requirements of the new management. The demands of the times are to provide individual managers, according to their function, with the information they must have if they are to discharge effectively their roles of administrator/planners and innovators. This is the opposite of routine data on past events possibly clouded by outdated accounting conventions. It is of increasing importance that the information be comprehensible to the manager concerned; for this purpose there is a great virtue in simplicity, a virtue often absent from accounting statements.

All this does not absolve the manager from understanding the fundamentals of accounting capabilities and limitations. But it does mean that the profession of accountancy must take a new and hard look at long-established procedures and conventions, and search for the simple truth rather than elaborate sophistication of business facts and possibilities. The business accountant must be prophet rather than historian.

Many accountants are acutely aware of the need to keep their art abreast of the current of business, and are actively engaged in debating the issues involved. The prolonged and, at the time of writing, unresolved controversy on inflation accounting is a case in point. The persistence of inflation, and the evident inability of conventional accounting to measure an unstable currency, have raised fundamental and disturbing questions as to the validity of hitherto sacrosanct accounting principles and concepts. The debate has extended inevitably beyond a discussion of the accurate measurement of wealth, to questions of the nature and measurement of profit, and hence to the meaning of cost. At the same time there is a growing recognition that the parallel and related concept of cash flow may be of equal importance to profit as a measure of success in business and may, indeed, be more comprehensible and acceptable to management.

The development of inflation accounting appears to have reinforced the well-established idea that there is a clear distinction between transactions on capital account and those on revenue account; this has highlighted the analogous but less precise distinction between profits and losses derived from normal trading and those derived from extraordinary occurrences. Inflation accounting has also caused questions to be revived regarding the real nature of the depreciation of wasting assets, but has not solved problems as to the treatment of other forms of deferred charges, such as research and development.

The recent preoccupation with the problems of inflation appears to have distracted attention from some other necessary developments in the art of providing management with effective information for the purposes of forward planning and control. For example, can accounting give no guidance to management on the complex problem of pricing policy, other than to prepare sometimes dubious statements of product cost? The validity of the unit cost has itself become questionable as a result of the continued increase in the proportion of business expenditure of an indirect nature and the extension of automatic processes. It may be that the most useful course to be taken by financial planning is to consider the totality of the business unit – its capacity to produce and sell, its pricing policy, the investment required, and the future cash inflows and outflows essential for the forward plan.

The production of an annual balance sheet is still regarded as the culminating point of the accounting exercise, although its limitations are widely recognized. In its conventional form, the balance sheet may at best foretoken impending insolvency, but it is of little use to the manager preoccupied with generating profit from sales. Nevertheless there remains a vital need for a regular and timely statement to be produced which (a) sets out the extent to which the planned financial position has been achieved and (b) indicates the financial resources available for the future.

For the purpose of controlling the financial consequences of their activities it is necessary that managers have at least a broad understanding of the principles, conventions and even the basic mechanics of accounting. There is no need for them to become involved in the technicalities but they should have sufficient knowledge to be able to question the applicability of the information provided for them. This fact underlies the foregoing discussion of the problems involved in the purposeful presentation of financial information about so complex an entity as a modern business. It also supports the following short chapter's description, in their elemental simplicity, of the manner in which the basic principles of accounting are applied.

1 Survey of accounting principles

In the introductory chapter it was suggested that the manager's prime function was to plan, not only forward but a long way forward, and to control the execution of the forward plans. It was also suggested that the main object of the accounting discipline was to aid management. If these premises are correct, it follows that accounting, side by side with management, must also be forward looking. Succeeding chapters of this book are concerned with financial techniques aimed at assisting managers to carry out their dual functions of planning and control. The present chapter discusses the accounting principles and conventions which are necessary for managers to understand if they are to make full and effective use of the management accounting service.

Every science or art has produced its conventions, the purpose of which is presumably to aid communication and understanding of the techniques used. Conventional symbols are used in mathematics; the sonnet is written in a conventional form, and there are well-established conventions in the art of ballet. So it is with accounting which in many ways is a form of expression and combines the characteristics of a science with those of an art. It is important to observe, however, that conventions of any art or science are in a state of continuous evolution, particularly in an era of rapid change, and that, at any given point of time, there exists a number of schools of thought as to the conventions which are most suitable to the conditions of the age.

It has been implied that the conventions of accounting emerge from the circumstances and needs of the times. From the most workable conventions certain principles evolve. Ideally, it may be argued that principles should be the basis of conventions, but the authors believe that in the infinitely complex world of business, the principles of accounting have evolved from careful analysis of the practice found to be most applicable to the facts.

Pursuing this line of thought, the following paragraphs attempt to extract the main principles inherent in current accounting conventions. It was stated earlier that accounting was not an exact science. It offers room for many viewpoints and differences of opinion, and it is perhaps desirable to mention here that some of the viewpoints expressed in the next section may not be acceptable to all accountants. The real question is whether they are acceptable to businessmen for whom accountants are providing a professional service; this is a question which is left to the reader to judge.

The first principle – *The business as an entity*

Contrary to common belief, the principles of accounting are comparatively few in number and quite simple to understand on the basis of common sense. One man or woman may be the sole owner of a business; a number of partners may own a firm; the shareholders are the owners of a limited liability company. In all these forms of organization the accounting records treat the business as an entity which is quite distinct from the owners, whether they be one or many. So far as the accounts are concerned it is the business which owns the assets and owes money to the creditors, the bank and the other lenders such as debenture holders. The capital of the business, in the widest sense of the term, is the figure arrived at by deducting the values of the assets as shown in the books from the value of the liabilities to external interests. Inherent in the accounting records is the assumption that the capital of the business is the sum due from the business to the owners. Capital, therefore, is in this sense another form of creditor.

If a person starts a business with, say, £100 in the bank, the accounts will record two aspects: (a) the asset of cash in the bank owned by the business and (b) the same amount due from the business to the owner, representing his capital. *A balance sheet* (which essentially records the final balances in the account), if drawn up immediately after the business has been created, will appear as follows:

Balance sheet

Owner's capital	£100	Cash at bank	£100

For a limited company or other corporate body, the sum due from the business to the proprietors (shareholders) will consist of the issued share capital, and additions to this original capital either from further funds subscribed by the shareholders or from retained profits, which are called reserves. The balance sheet of a limited company, reduced to its essentials and prepared some time after the company has been created, might be presented on the lines shown below.

In essence, this statement shows that the company owns assets of £266,000 and owes to outside interests £66,000, a net sum of £200,000 being the capital of the company, representing a conventional liability to the shareholders. The same figure is arrived at by adding together the issued capital, the general reserve, and the undistributed profits (the *profit and loss account*).

XYZ Company Limited

Balance sheet as at 31 December 19..

Issued capital			*Fixed assets* (at cost *less* depreciation)		
Ordinary shares		£150,000			
			Land and buildings	£100,000	
Revenue reserves			Plant and machinery	60,000	
			Other fixed assets	20,000	
General reserve	£45,000				£180,000
Profit and loss a/c	5,000		*Current assets*		
			Cash	£6,000	
			Debtors	30,000	
		50,000	Stocks	50,000	
Current liabilities		£200,000			86,000
Creditors	£40,000				
Taxation	26,000				
		66,000			
		£266,000			£266,000

As a result of the operation of the first principle that the business is a separate entity from the owners, the total liabilities of the business (comprising the amounts due to external interests and the capital due to the shareholders) are always equal to the total assets, so far as the accounts are concerned. Every profit made is an additional value which belongs to the shareholders and is added to the profit and loss account or to the reserves until and unless it is paid out to the shareholders by way of dividends. Of course, the capital subscribed by the shareholders, as distinct from the profits due to them, cannot normally be paid back to them until the company is dissolved.

It follows from the principle under discussion that owners' capital always equals assets less external liabilities. This aspect of the accounting principle is more clearly illustrated by the form of balance sheet adopted by many companies which shows, first, the sources of the funds used in the business (alternatively described as *capital employed*) and, secondly, the manner in which those funds have been employed (alternatively called *employment of the capital*). Drawn up in such a form the foregoing balance sheet would appear as on page 21.

It is recognized that the foregoing will be familiar to most readers. But the importance of refreshing one's thinking about the subject under discussion in this section is that the ultimate objective of the forward-planning exercise is to produce a financial position which is an improvement on the position when the planning begins. The profit made by a business will be reflected in the balance sheet, and more particularly in the capital due to the proprietors, until it is paid out to them in whole or in part. Many shareholders and many teams of management are more concerned with the growth of the business, tantamount to augmenting the shareholders' capital, than with the distribution of large profits by way of dividened. The balance sheet, especially that part which represents the shareholders' interests in the business, reflects the success or failure of the planning and control, and in this sense is the final measure of efficient management.

Sources of the funds			
(*Capital employed*)			
Issued ordinary shares			£150,000
Revenue reserves			
General reserve		£45,000	
Profit and loss account		5,000	
			50,000
			£200,000

Application of the funds			
(*Employment of the capital*)			
Fixed assets			
Land and buildings		£100,000	
Plant and machinery		60,000	
Other fixed assets		20,000	
			£180,000
Current assets			
Cash		£6,000	
Debtors		30,000	
Stocks		50,000	
Current liabilities		£86,000	
Creditors	£40,000		
Taxation due	26,000		
		66,000	
			20,000
			£200,000

Limitations of the balance sheet The balance sheet is normally regarded as a historical document, that is, as a statement of what *was* the financial position of a business at a point of time; it has been likened to a snapshot photograph of the business at that moment in time. This book, on the other hand, is concerned with the future. The balance sheet may have a value for forward planning – indicating the resources available for planning the future activities of the business – but its value for these purposes will diminish as time passes and it becomes outdated. Substantial change can occur in both the internal finances and the external circumstances of a business within a month, so rapid are the processes of change in the modern world. Unfortunately for most large businesses and, indeed, some smaller ones, the demands of detailed accuracy and the legal requirement of an audit may mean that the balance sheet drawn up to conform with the requirements of the Companies Acts takes months to prepare. It will consequently be of very little use as a basis for the forward plan.

It is true that the process of preparing the annual accounts can be speeded up by the aid of interim accounting procedures, perpetual inventories, continuous auditing and other devices, aided by computerization. When it is appreciated that many of the values shown in the balance sheet (especially for fixed assets and stocks) are more the outcome of intelligent judgement in relation to future events than absolute amounts, then some of the time and energy spent on the niceties of valuations can be avoided. Even so, the exercise of formulating the forward plan, which needs to involve all the major operational areas of the business, is unlikely to be completed in less than a month. Thus the process must be initiated well before the starting date when the plan is to be in effect.

The planners will need to base their forecasts on such internal information as the cash available in the business and what can be obtained, the state of the debtors and creditors, and the availability of stocks. In addition the planners will certainly need to consider current trends in expenses and in the profitability of sales lines. For the purpose of the operational plans, the value at which fixed assets are shown in the accounts is largely irrelevant. Likewise long-term investments and capital funds are of little interest in formulating the operational plans, although such items may be of importance for aspects of financial planning. Thus, that part of the balance sheet which is of particular interest in formulating the forecasts of cash flow, investment, income and expenditure, is the conglomeration of items embraced by the description *net current assets.* This simplifies the balance sheet information required by the planners. There is no need for them to await the compilation of formalized accounts; the items in which they are concerned can be forecast from a previous balance sheet, especially if these statements are prepared at frequent intervals, preferably monthly, and are close to the point in time to which they relate.

One figure which is important for forward planning, and which can only be derived from the complete balance sheet, is the amount of capital employed in the business. This figure may be ascertained by adding together the total of the share capital, the loan capital and the reserves, or alternatively by deducting amounts due to external interests, such as trade creditors, from the total assets. Profit in relation to capital employed is usually regarded as the overall measure of success, but the figure of capital employed depends on the basis on which the assets are valued, especially the fixed assets and stocks. These values are traditionally based on what the assets originally cost. In the case of stocks, particularly of work in progress, the value depends largely on the method used in applying overheads to direct cost; the outcome of that exercise in turn depends on convention and judgement. Thus there is no such thing as the absolute cost of an item of work in progress or of finished stock. The discussion of the effect of inflation on accounting data has thrown considerable doubt as to the validity of using historical cost as the basis of valuing both stock and fixed assets. Should these assets be valued at, for example, their value to the business or at the current cost of replacing them? If the true value of the assets held by a business is a matter of controversy, so is the value of the capital which it employs. One of the many implications of the controversy about inflation is the question of the validity of measuring a company's profit in relation to the capital employed in producing that profit.

The problem of the valuation of capital employed is, however, one which refers to the measurement of the profitability of the company as a whole. The managers concerned with the financial aspects of operational planning, in essence output and sales, are dealing with a large number of discrete investments of funds; for example, investments in projects of development, new plant, new sales outlets, new products. It is the sum total of a large miscellany of projects which constitutes the total company activity.

It should be possible to ascertain the additional amount of money which will be required by each of these projects, and to relate expected profit from each project to the funds which it employs. It is not past spending sunk into the company which is in question for the purpose of forward planning, but rather the future expenditure incurred by company activities, and which will be released from internal sources within the company or obtained from outside. This is not to say that the planner can evade the influence of inflation, but he is concerned with the inflation which will occur in the future, not that which has occurred in the past.

The second principle – *Double entry*

The concept of the business as a separate entity entails the keeping of accounts on the so-called 'double-entry principle'. This means, in short, that every transaction is entered twice in the accounts, because, for example, the acquisition of an asset involves either the loss of another asset (e.g. cash) or an addition to the liabilities of the business, either to outside creditors or to the owners. Additional funds brought into the business by the owners (e.g. an issue of more shares) have two effects: (a) to increase the liability of the business to the owners by the amount of the additional funds subscribed and (b) to increase the assets of the company, in this case in the form of additional cash. Thus every transaction has two functions in the accounting system.

It would be quite possible to construct reasonably effective accounts without using the double-entry principle. Such accounts would comprise records of assets acquired and liabilities incurred to persons outside the business. The interest of the owners in the business could then be ascertained by deducting the assets from the liabilities. Such a system would have two demerits. It would not be possible to segregate the interests of the owners into their constituent parts – issued capital, capital reserves, revenue reserves, and profit and loss account. Secondly, the automatic check conferred by the double-entry system would be absent.

The application of the double-entry system imposes a certain rigidity on account keeping. It means, for example, that when an asset such as stock is bought from a creditor, the gain in the form of the asset must be shown as equal to the loss represented by the amount owing to the creditor. Whilst the amount owing to the creditor is normally a fact which can be recorded precisely, the value gained by the purchase is certainly not the *same* amount, or the purchase would not have been made. Whether it is desirable or even possible to adopt a system of account keeping different from the double-entry system (which has worked tolerably well for nearly 500 years) must be extremely doubtful, but at the same time the limitations imposed by the system need to be understood. It is largely as a result of double entry that accounts are traditionally recorded in terms of original cost and, without complex adaptations, the resulting figures take no account of changing money values. Such adaptations have been recommended for inflation accounting.

It is not the purpose of this book to examine the mechanics of double entry, but it is desirable that the reader shall understand the essentials of the system; for the forward plans of the management are going to be expressed finally in a manner which conforms to the double-entry principle. The elements of double entry may perhaps be most succinctly shown by the use of a simple matrix. For this purpose we refer to the first illustration of a business which was started with £100 in the bank. Assume that £20 of the capital was immediately disbursed by paying wages of this amount; that stock was bought on credit for £50; that £60 of furniture was bought for cash; and that sales of stock which cost £10 to buy were made on credit for £15. The double aspect of each transaction might be shown by the following matrix.

The figures at the bottom of the vertical columns are the liabilities of the business after the transactions have been made and those at the right-hand end of the horizontal rows are the assets. The final position could be shown by a conventional balance sheet in the following manner:

Balance sheet

Owner's capital	£85	Cash	£20
		Stock	40
		Debtors	15
Creditors	50	Furniture	60
	£135		£135

Liabilities and deductions from assets

Assets and deductions from liabilities	Owner's capital	Creditors	Cash	Stock	Totals	Deduct transfers	Final assets
Cash	100				100	80	20
Stock		50			50	10	40
Furniture			60		60	—	60
Debtors	15				15	—	15
Owner's capital			20 (wages)	10	30	30	—
Totals	115	50	80	10			
Transfers	30	—	80	10			
Final liabilities	85	50	—	—			135

The matrix system of recording would be unwieldy in practice but does serve to illustrate the essential two-sided aspect of accounting entries. Readers who wish to learn more about the mechanics of accounting are referred to the many excellent text-books on the subject, particularly to *Finance and Accounts for Managers* by Desmond Goch, also published in this series.

The third principle – *Capital v. Revenue*

In the last section capital was defined as the difference between the assets of a business and the external liabilities. It is, however, necessary to point out that a variety of other meanings are attributed to the term *capital*. For instance, the issued shares are often referred to as 'the capital of the company', although in fact they form only part of the capital as the expression is used in the present context. What we are discussing is capital in the sense of the whole of the net assets which are used for the purpose of earning income. This concept is often termed *net worth*, although the latter expression conveys an incorrect implication that the net assets as shown in the accounts represent the price that would be paid for the company in the open market. The balance sheet figures, and hence the capital of a company, are basically a statement of the funds which are employed in a business and how they have been applied; they are not in any sense a statement of current values.

In a successful business the funds will have been applied to the acquisition of assets, some of which (the fixed assets) will have been acquired to aid the earning process; others, the stock and work-in-progress, will have been acquired or produced for sale; and the remainder, the debtors and cash, represent the proceeds of sales. There will be, in addition, idle funds held as cash at the bank or in investments, representing money awaiting application. Whatever the detail, the ultimate object is to dispose of the stock for a greater sum than was originally expended in acquiring it. Thus, a business is concerned with adding value to the original investment, and the added value is profit. In a simple retailing business the process may be depicted as follows:

Investment of cash

Acquisition of goods for resale

Values added to the goods
(through services provided by the retailer)

Disposal of the goods at the added values

Receipt of cash for the goods sold

Purchase of further goods or services

Distribution of profit to the owners

In a manufacturing business the value added to the raw materials acquired takes the form of labour and overheads in the factory, plus marketing and administrative expenses and financing costs.

In most companies, however, the process of adding values is limited to the factory costs, primarily for reasons of prudent accounting.

It would be possible to operate an accounting system which recorded only assets and liabilities, and the changes therein. However, the managers of a business need also to have analyses of the transactions which have caused increases or decreases in the capital, the purpose of such analyses being to draw lessons from past errors in planning future activities. It is these analyses of movements in the assets which are recorded in the revenue accounts and eventually summarized in the form of a profit and loss account, and its subsidiary schedules. It is important to appreciate that the profit and loss account merely measures the value of additions to capital in the form of sales and other income, and the losses of capital in the form of the cost of the goods sold, and the selling and administrative expenses.

From this viewpoint the idea that there are two kinds of transaction, capital and revenue, is unreal. All the activities of the business are of a capital nature, because they either add to or detract from the capital. Revenue accounts *per se* measure the extent of the increases or losses of capital. The payment of wages, for example, is often described as a payment on revenue account, but in fact the wages paid to the operatives either increase the value of the work in progress on the factory floor or, if they create no value, they are losses of capital. Wages are, therefore, essentially of a capital nature. The same argument could be applied to the indirect expenses which add value to the work-in-progress through the overhead rate applied to output.

The vital point of this discussion is that it is false and misleading to attempt to segregate the transactions of a business into the so-called revenue and capital categories. All transactions affect the capital of the business; all have the objective of increasing the capital. Some achieve this objective and some fail to do so. There is a distinction, however, between capital and revenue accounts. The accounts which *record* acquisitions of assets and liabilities are the capital accounts; those which *measure* the increase or decrease in capital are the revenue accounts. It is the revenue accounts which are summarized in the form of a profit and loss account and which inform the management of the extent to which capital has been increased or reduced; the revenue accounts measure the increase or decrease in capital caused by the main groups of transactions.

What is popularly meant by a 'transaction on capital account' is in fact the acquisition of a fixed asset, i.e., the acquisition of an asset which is not primarily held for resale but to aid the profit-earning process, such as the purchase of a machine or factory buildings. Conversely a 'transaction on revenue account' signifies either the proceeds of the sale of stock or services, or the values which have been added to create the stock or services. One of the values which is added is the cost of the machinery and other fixed assets; for such costs are spread forward over the expected life of the asset by means of the depreciation charge. They enter into the calculation of overhead rates, and thus form costs similar to wages or general overheads. Even the distinction between a 'fixed asset' and a 'current asset' is simply one dependent on the time which will elapse before the asset is consumed in the course of the business activities.

This discussion, theoretical and academic as it may first appear, is essential groundwork for the later consideration of the forward-planning process because forward planning consists largely of planning means of increasing values. Considerable attention has recently been paid to the subject of capital budgeting, and the layman is led to believe that it is some important form of budgeting which is distinct from all other forms of budgeting. This is just not true. If this book has a single theme it is that all budgeting for a business concern is capital budgeting, in the sense that all budgeting is the planning of expenditure directed to the production of increased values in the future.

The fourth principle – *Matching expenditure against income*

The layman unused to the conventions of accounting may quite logically conclude that when a business has spent, say, £20 on producing an article or service which will sell for £25, then the capital of the business has increased by £5; in other words a profit of £5 has been made. To the accountant, however, no profit will arise before the goods have been dispatched to the customer. Furthermore, if the accountant is doubtful whether the full price of £25 will be received from the customer he may further defer the recording of the profit until the cash for the goods is actually received by the business. The practice of deferring profit in this manner is a convention of accounting which has a sound basis in prudency, but it means that profit does not appear in the accounts until long after the effort has been made which produced the profit.

From this practical basis the principle has been evolved that expenditure must be matched against the income which that expenditure produces. In applying this principle, the full values which have been accumulated (for example, the full value of manufactured stock) are not recorded in the accounting system until the goods have been sold or the services supplied and accepted by the customer. The values being added to work in progress in the workshops of a manufacturing business are rarely the full values; they represent transfers of portions of the business capital from one lot to another. Thus, the booking of an operative's time on jobs results in the accountant increasing the value of the work in progress by the (approximate) amount of wages paid to the operative for his time; it also involves a reduction in cash when the wages are paid – that is, a transfer from the asset cash to the asset work in progress. When stock is bought from a supplier, a liability to the supplier is created in the accounts and the value of stock is increased by an equivalent amount. Eventually the supplier is paid, so that in this instance a transfer of capital has also to be made from the asset cash to the asset stock. A similar operation occurs when works services are incorporated in an overhead rate which is applied to jobs for the purpose of increasing their value in the accounts. The full values created by the business are not recorded in the accounts until the stock is delivered to the customer.

It has already been suggested that accounting principles are often derived from the most effective practices. It follows that strict adherence to principles must be severely modified by circumstances. A qualification to the principle of matching expenditure against the income which that expenditure produces occurs in the accounting treatment of administration and marketing expenses. These are the expenses which are not considered to have arisen in the factory or department where the production of the goods or services is carried out. The expenses of a business may be broadly classified as those which are incurred in producing the goods or services, in selling the products, and in administering the business as such. Clearly, these classifications are closely interrelated.

It is customary in most but not all businesses to 'write off' administrative and marketing expenses against the income of the period in which those expenses were incurred. Thus, the costs of selling, advertising and administration shown in the accounts may have little if any relevance to the sales shown in the same set of accounts. This lack of precise correlation between income and expenses becomes emphasized in the short term, e.g. when monthly, quarterly, or half-yearly accounts are produced. It will also be true in the longer term when a heavy investment is made in, say, sales promotion and administrative systems to meet the needs of future development.

The convention of writing off marketing and administration expenses as they are incurred is another example of the prudent view inherent in accounting practice. There can be little doubt that prudent accounting is not only justified but also essential in view of the incurable optimism of most business managers. The reader will be aware of several business 'crashes' of recent years which occurred because the acounting was not prudent enough.

Nevertheless, there seems to be little logic, in principle, in failing to match marketing and administrative expenses against the income they are designed to produce, or at least in treating them as values to be added to the stock they have helped to produce or sell. It is noteworthy that many companies dealing largely in government contract work (which is fundamentally a question of calculating a price which will recover all applicable costs plus a percentage profit) do, in fact, include administrative and some marketing expenses in the overhead rate applied to work in progress.

Business is to some extent conducted on a basis of expediency – accounting techniques must follow suit. But it is important to observe that, because of the conventions mentioned above, the profits shown by a business do not coincide in time with the efforts made to produce those profits.

The points already made may be illustrated by the following fairly typical, although hypothetical, form of trading and profit and loss account used by many large companies for the information of management.

Summarized revenue account

for the month of January

	Sales		£500,000
Less:	Cost of goods sold		300,000
	Gross profit		£200,000
Less:	Expenses –		
	Warehousing	£15,000	
	Distribution	20,000	
	Selling	30,000	
	Advertising	50,000	
	Administration	25,000	
	Total expenses		140,000
	Operating profit		£60,000
Less:	Non-trading items		5,000
	Pretax profit		£55,000
	Tax provision		22,000
	Net profit after tax		£33,000

It will be apparent from the above example that the principle of matching expenditure against the income to which that expenditure relates extends only to the factory cost of the goods sold. Even the selling costs were probably aimed at making sales in future months. Thus, the £300,000 shown as the cost of the goods sold will be quite a different figure from the expenditure incurred in the month in the factory during the period in question.

The expenditure chargeable to the factory might consist of the following transactions:

Direct costs		
(Those chargeable to the work-in progress without undue apportionment)		
Raw materials used	£60,000	
Bought out parts	20,000	
Wages of operatives	80,000	
Total direct costs		£160,000
Indirect (overhead) costs		
Supervision	£40,000	
Indirect labour	30,000	
Consumable stores	15,000	
Works services	55,000	
Depreciation of plant	60,000	
Total indirect costs		200,000
Total costs of production		£360,000

The £360,000 represents the values added in the workshop during the period. To ascertain the values put into finished goods store, the following sum is carried out:

Work in progress in the factory at the beginning of the period	£60,000
Values added in the period	360,000
	£420,000
Work in progress remaining at the end of the period	40,000
Values added to finished goods store	£380,000

To find the cost of the goods sold involves the following further sum:

Values in finished goods store at the beginning of the period	£900,000
Values added by deliveries from the factory	380,000
	£1,280,000
Less: Values remaining in store at the end of the period	980,000
Cost of goods sold	£300,000

The fifth principle – *Usage*

Although £360,000 was shown in the previous section as being chargeable to the factory as added values during the period, this amount does not represent the expenditure actually incurred by the factory. The raw material cost of £60,000 was the cost of the materials used and the actual purchases incurred during the period may have been much more or much less. Likewise, the depreciation of the plant is an estimate of the proportion of the plant cost used up in the period; it is possible that a very much higher figure was incurred for plant acquired. So far as the expenses are concerned, the figures shown in the factory account were the result of making adjustments to the actual amount incurred for prepayments, provisions, and accrued expenses. Thus, it may be that in the period the advertising expenditure incurred was, say, £150,000 but it was considered that only £50,000 referred to this period of account. Some of the expenditure shown would have been incurred in previous periods; and some may be provisions for charges not yet incurred.

It follows, therefore, that in addition to matching expenditure against income the accountant endeavours to relate expenditure to accounting periods, by assessing the extent to which the goods or services acquired were actually used up in the period. It is, in fact, this latter process which normally precedes the matching of the resultant expenditure against the income of the period. It might be said that the two processes have much the same objective but there are many items of expense charged in a period which were never incurred to earn income, but which represent usage of assets and services, e.g. the cost of idle machinery, redundancy pay and other employee benefits. Where standard costing is used the writing off of variances when they are incurred is, in effect, an extension of the usage principle.

The application of the principles to forward planning and control

The importance of the foregoing examination of accounting principles and conventions is that they are as applicable to the forward-planning process as they are to the recording of the results. The management plan will be designed fundamentally to increase the liability of the business to the owners by adding values to the store of net assets. The plans of the managers and of the management team as a whole must eventually be formalized on accounting principles; firstly, because success in business is customarily measured by the process of applying those principles; secondly, because any comparison between plans and results (which is the precursor to control) will clearly be valid only if both subjects for comparison are drawn up on the same conventions and use the same language.

This means that the plans will need to be expressed in the form of forward accounts, both those of a capital nature – the budgeted assets and liabilities – and those of a revenue nature – the analysis of the gains and losses of capital. In preparing the budgets the planned profit will emerge only after budgeted expenditure has been matched against budgeted income and after the cost of goods and services which are likely to be used up in the forward activities has been written off against income and applied to the correct period of forward accounts. It will, in addition, be particularly important in forward planning for careful consideration to be given to the anticipated timing of expenditure likely to be incurred and to the timing of cash payments and receipts, for the availability of cash will be the overriding limiting factor in any form of forward planning.

The mounting need for long-range planning in industry has been mentioned earlier. When a business is considering plans for, perhaps, twenty years hence, the question must arise as to whether existing accounting conventions will be adequate for the future conditions in which business is to be conducted. Searching questions have been asked for some years past as to whether the accountancy profession has been able adequately to reflect in its accounting systems the effect of changing monetary values. There is no evidence that money values will achieve stability in the foreseeable future. Is the basis of accounting, which deals essentially with cash paid and cash received on a so-called 'historical' formula, adequate to modern and foreseeable conditions? Should the expenditure which is matched against income in a profit and loss account be the cost of the materials, machinery and services used, or the cost of replacing this stock of capital? In a fully automated factory will it be possible to continue the process of matching expenditure against income, or to say how much of a particular item of expenditure, such as depreciation, maintenance and services, relate to certain sales? These are some of the questions which merit the careful attention of managers and these are the questions we propose to consider in greater detail in this book.

2 The basis of the forward plan

Objectives and policy

Financial planning must be directed to aiding management in achieving its objectives and in fulfilling its policy. Both the scope of the objectives and the nature of the policy may well be limited by financial considerations. Consequently, it is of prime importance that both objectives and policy should be clearly stated, so that it shall be apparent at the beginning whether their fulfilment is likely to be limited by questions of cost and the availability of cash. It is also important that objectives and policy shall be communicated to the managers, as far 'down the line' as is practicable, so that the plans of the various departments shall conform to corporate policy.

Management literature is full of glib phrases about the need for clear definitions of objectives and policy, but the very familiarity of those words tends to blunt their meaning. Most businessmen would state their objective with brevity: *to make profits.* Despite the tendency in some circles to regard profit almost as an objectionable word, it is difficult to fault the single-minded pursuit of profit – qualified, of course, as it normally is, by ethical standards. Certainly financial planning is largely concerned with profit.

Profit may thus be considered to be the first objective of business. In view of the heavy investment needed to ensure the success of most enterprises, profit tends to become the long-term objective; at least, the *realization* of the profit in accounting terms must await the development not only of the product but also of the market. Peter Drucker has pointed out in *The Practice of Management* (published in this series) that the economist's conception of the maximization of profit no longer applies; a business is concerned with 'the minimum profit needed for survival'. He is probably, however, referring to the larger business. For the small concern, which is frequently in a semi-monopoly position, the objective may well be to maximize profits. The small concern, with a monopoly of product, service or area of operations, will tend to maximize profits until it emerges into a large concern fighting for survival in a highly competitive market; and then it will be aiming for the minimum profit necessary for survival. The small concern may find its monopoly under attack from a larger business. The most obvious example is where the small shopkeeper finds he is losing sales to a near-by supermarket. In such a situation the small man will still seek to maximize the profit from what remains of his turnover, perhaps by increasing his price and improving his service, until he eventually succumbs or is taken over.

Even though profit may be the first objective, all businesses have a number of ancillary objectives, and these objectives need identifying if an integrated plan of operations is to be established. The fact must be faced that the objectives of a business frequently reflect the attitudes, desires and limitations of the man who can command the greatest voting power at the annual meetings. Other matters which affect objectives are location of the business, financial strength, customer goodwill, even a policy of fulfilling national needs, and sometimes reasoned argument by the management team.

Depending, therefore, on the personalities and the circumstances of a business, it may have, at any one time, a number of objectives, but each of them should be subordinate to the need for long-term profitability. Each objective will still have some bearing on financial planning and should be given due weight in carrying out that vital exercise of management. Furthermore, objectives may change – they will inevitably change – in relation to the rapidly changing world in which we live.

With such considerations in mind, the kind of objectives with which this book will be primarily concerned are those of growth, development overseas, diversification, rationalization of the product line, automation of manufacturing and administrative processes, and the more obvious and popular objective of obtaining a larger share of the available market. For a well-established company which already controls a large market share, the objective may well be to expand the total market.

Despite the overall need for long-term profitability, the kind of objectives indicated above may well become more dominant in the short-term planning operations than profitability. Whatever the situation in a particular business, two requirements with regard to objectives are outstanding: the first that the top management be clear as to what these objectives are, both for short- and long-term purposes; the second that the objectives which are formulated by superior management be communicated to subordinate managers at all practical levels. Communication of objectives is a *sine qua non* of a harmonious framework of planning.

So much for the objectives. The next word in the title to this section which requires explanation is *policy*, by which is meant the policy to be adopted for achieving the objectives. If the objectives of a business can be numerous, methods of policy can have infinite variety; but, again, clear communication to all levels of management is vital. By policy we mean also such matters as timing: the time when an entry into overseas markets is to be achieved; the question of whether an entry into a new market is to be accomplished by a breakthrough at one point of time or by more gradual penetration; whether prices are to start low with a view to discouraging competition, and then to be raised, or whether they are to start high and be lowered to meet competition.

Personnel policy, especially in relation to rationalization or automation, will always be important, and must be decided in advance of the events.

Organization policy, likewise, must be laid down to meet the objectives; expansion may for example necessitate decentralization, whilst rationalization may require a contrary process so far as organization is concerned.

It is difficult to conceive of a policy decision which will not have financial repercussions. So far as the few examples given above are concerned, entry into overseas markets will involve fundamental decisions on the financial problems of credit control, exchange risks and the provision of funds. Any form of contraction of the labour force will necessitate careful financial planning in relation to the incidence of redundancy payments and compensation. Decentralization and its converse involve intricate financial problems of costing, budgeting, and financial control. Certainly, the financial problems of automation represent a new field of investigation for the business accountant.

Insufficient attention is generally given in business to the two essential preliminaries of forward planning: the formulation and statement of objectives and policies. One reason appears to be the hand-to-mouth methods adopted in many concerns; another is the reluctance to state objectives in case they are not achieved, thereby involving 'loss of face'. Hand-to-mouth management may have achieved some successes during the period when the preoccupation of business in this country was to meet demand; nowadays the preoccupation must be how to meet worldwide competition. Timidity in the business world of the future is the sure road to inevitable failure.

The profit target – the return on capital

It is a truism that capital is invested in business to yield a return. What interests the investor is the rate of return and the risk; if he concludes that the risk is great he will require a greater return. The return in this sense is not necessarily dividends, or cash flow. Many investors, both individuals and institutions, are looking for a return as much in increased capital values as in dividends. The difficulty, of course, lies in quantifying the risk and assessing the required return in relation to the capital invested. It is also a question, as argued above, of quantifying the capital employed, especially to the extent that it is affected by changing money values. The investor regards his capital as that sum which he could realize if he sold his shares or debentures, and in theory he should always be considering whether he could obtain a greater return on that sum with equal risk. Thus, if the company wishes to maintain the market values of its shares and debentures – particularly important when the time comes to issue further capital – the company as well as the investor must have regard to the rate of return, or yield, on the market capitalization of the securities. This consideration should influence the profit target to be established by the company. In this respect the interests of the investor and those of the business are identical. In a sense the whole art of business lies in evaluating the risk. Mathematical devices can help, but in the end the vital qualities required are those of knowledge, experience, sometimes flair, but always a carefully thought-out plan and an efficient mechanism for controlling the execution of the plan.

Even if it is difficult for a particular business to assess the rate of interest which will represent insurance against risk, it is nevertheless not difficult to establish the minimum return which a business must achieve in the long run. The minimum return is the rate of interest which could be earned on the capital employed if it were invested elsewhere without appreciable risk. The rate of return on undated government securities such as 2½% Consols, which is of course considerably higher than 2½%, can be used to represent the minimum rate of return for most practical purposes, although this rate has fluctuated considerably over the years. It is interesting to note that some of the largest UK companies earn no more than the minimum.

The argument so far is that the first three essentials of successful planning are:

1 To establish objectives.
2 To formulate policy for achieving the objectives.
3 To calculate profit target.

The profit target will consist of at least two elements: firstly, the minimum profit required to justify the existence of the business and, secondly, insurance against risk. In fact, of course, if opportunities present themselves businessmen may feel justified in aiming at profits much greater than are required to cover the two elements of interest and risk. In an intensely competitive world, however, many businesses find themselves struggling to achieve the minimum return; if this is the case, it is the profit target which will rightly determine the nature and scope of the operations. The need to achieve the profit target should stimulate efforts to expand, rationalize, diversify, improve pricing policy, decentralize, or carry out any of the innumerable policy devices which are available to a business in its unending search for optimum efficiency. Because of its importance, the nature of the profit target for a business merits further examination.

For *capital-intensive companies* the profit target must be a long-term aim. *Long term* means here a period of at least five years, possibly longer. The competitive world demands increasing investment not only in plant and machinery but also in research, development, training, marketing and administrative systems. Very rarely can the money spent on such investment be recovered within a year or so. The expression capital intensive usually implies a business with a large proportion of its capital invested in plant. But if the meaning is widened to embrace other forms of investment, then it appears that the tendency for even non-manufacturing companies is for them to become increasingly capital intensive as they grow. Thus, as noted above, the period of planning is daily becoming extended, and consequently the period covered by a profit target must be extended likewise.

In short, it is often a more practical proposition to say that a business must aim to achieve a certain figure of profit over, say, five years, than a fifth of this figure in any one year. During the progress of the planning period the business may have to suffer lean periods whilst it is contending with cyclical depressions, changes in taste and fashion, and technological advances.

In assessing the required profit target, for whatever period it is aimed to cover, two very real problems arise: (a) quantifying the capital to which the desired rate of return is to be applied and (b) defining the nature of 'profit'. No special problems occur in quantifying the invested capital of a new enterprise, for this is simply the initial money with which it is financed. If, for instance, £5 million is required to establish a subsidiary in, say, Australia, and the return required is 10%, then the initial profit target, expressed as an annual figure, is £500,000. But after the subsidiary has been operating for a year or so, the capital employed will change due to profits retained or losses incurred, to appreciation or depreciation of fixed assets, and to any further capital invested. Profit, as shown above, is not basically the result of some accounting mystique in preparing a profit and loss account, but is the result of valuing the assets and liabilities. Thus, the profit target which moulds the nature of the enterprise will depend on annual or more frequent valuations of assets and liabilities. A further problem, which will be considered in some detail later, is whether the profit should account for the changing purchasing power of money, that is inflation or deflation.

The figures in the conventional balance sheet represent little more than the costs which have not yet been set off against income and they are not therefore adequate without adjustment as a basis for calculating the capital invested in an enterprise for the purpose of establishing the profit required. A machine which has been substantially depreciated in the accounts may be worth almost as much to the business, as a source of profit, as when it was new. Accounting conventions prescribe, for good reasons, that stocks must be valued at no more than cost (and, where inflation accounting is applied, this may be replacement cost) and they will accordingly appear in the balance sheet at well below their saleable value or their value as profit-earning assets. Similarly, patents, trade marks and goodwill may be of much greater potential value to the business than is shown by the figure, if any, by which they are represented in the balance sheet.

One could take the view, probably wrongly, that changes in money values are immaterial in deciding the profit an industrial enterprise ought to make. The return to the investor, if this view is taken, is properly based on historical cost. The profit target should be expressed as a percentage of original capital plus retained profits; current values of assets, even if they are ascertainable, are irrelevant. Inflation is a common loss to everyone, and there is no reason why the supplies of capital should be immune from its effects.

The fallacy of this argument can be demonstrated by instancing the situation of a property investment company. Assume that the last balance sheet contained the following summarized figures:

Capital employed	
Issued ordinary shares	£4,000,000
Revenue reserves	3,000,000
	£7,000,000

Employment of the capital

Properties, at cost less depreciation	£6,000,000
Net current assets	1,000,000
	£7,000,000

Assuming an expected rate of return on the above capital employed of 15% the annual profit target would be £1,050,000. Assuming that the properties were acquired many years ago their current saleable value would have increased considerably over cost, say to £9,000,000. A revalued balance sheet would then appear as follows:

Capital employed

Issued ordinary shares		£4,000,000
Reserves:		
surplus on the revaluation of properties	£3,000,000	
revenue reserves	3,000,000	
		6,000,000
		£10,000,000

Employment of the capital

Properties, at valuation	£9,000,000
Net current assets	1,000,000
	£10,000,000

Assuming that the investors could get 15% on their money elsewhere at equal risk, they would soon take steps to sell the properties or liquidate the company, and thus achieve a return of £1,500,000, rather than accept £1,050,000 from the existing management.

The example is oversimplified, for it uses a type of asset which is normally realizable at above cost. In the case of an industrial company, the plant may not even fetch the figures standing in the books if it were sold; the work in progress may be valueless in the open market. The real question is: what are the assets currently worth in terms of earning capacity? Or, to put the question in the opposite form: by how much would the profits fall if the asset did not exist, and what is the capital value of such loss?

The profit target – the valuation of earning capacity

The main reason why a business considers the purchase of a machine or other fixed asset is that it will either (a) increase the profits of the business or (b) prevent a fall in profits. In many cases an enterprise will acquire a machine simply because without the machine the business can no longer compete in a particular market; and no precise estimates of profit added or profit saved are made. Without some attempt at quantifying the merits of an acquisition of equipment, however, it is quite possible that the capital expenditure involved could have been put to a more remunerative purpose. Whilst the calculation may be subject to many assumptions, every piece of equipment acquired by a company should be subjected to a test of profitability.

Once the net income likely to be derived from the acquisition of plant has been estimated, the next question that arises is whether the expenditure is likely to be worthwhile; in other words, is the acquisition likely to satisfy the test of profitability? The simplest means of determining this is to assume that the net income to be derived will represent additional cash receipts flowing into the business. This assumption will not be entirely true within a particular time period taken within the life of the equipment because the incidence of profit does not necessarily synchronize with the incidence of cash flow. Nevertheless, over the whole period of the life of an asset the additional profit which it produces will be close to the cash flow.

The foregoing argument suggests that the real worth of an item of plant to a business is the present value of the net cash flow which it is likely to produce. Further examination of this concept is contained in the later section on capital budgeting, but for present purposes it is necessary to point out that the present value of the cash flow emanating from an asset is likely to be well above the original cost and certainly above the cost less depreciation. If this were not so the acquisition of the equipment in the first place would not have been justified. Furthermore, it is apparent that many pieces of equipment which have been considerably written down by depreciation in the business accounts are still very valuable assets in terms of earning capacity.

At this juncture it is desirable to point out that the present value of, say, £1,000 due in two years' time is £857, assuming that 8% per annum interest could be earned. In other words, at that rate of interest £857 receivable now is just as valuable as £1,000 due in two years' time, because £857 will accumulate to £1,000 in the period:

	Present	£857
Add:	Interest @ 8%	69
	One year	£926
Add:	Interest @ 8%	74
	Two years	£1,000

The present values of cash flows at various rates of interest and for different time periods may be calculated without difficulty by the use of discounting tables.

If the earning potential of assets is most scientifically represented by the present value of the cash flow which it is expected to generate, it follows that it is the present value also of the expected cash flow which is the logical basis for the valuation of the capital for the purpose of the calculation of a profit target for a business. However, it is absurd to imagine that a business could afford the time and effort involved in an annual calculation of the expected cash flow from each asset! Such an exercise might well be undertaken for specific groups of assets, but as a general rule the exercise is quite impracticable, whatever its theoretical advantages. It is, however, desirable that the true worth of business assets be borne in mind, especially as a standard against which to measure the validity of the more practical but less scientific alternatives discussed below.

The methods used in practice for bringing asset values more into line with current monetary values fall broadly under two headings, revalorization and revaluation. The method which has become known as *revalorization* consists of the application to balance sheet values of an index number which represents the change in value. Whilst revalorization has the appearance of scientific accuracy, in fact, when it is analysed, certain severe qualifications as to its validity appear. The first problem is the choice of index number to be used. The indices which are currently available for this purpose consist of indices of wholesale prices, of retail prices (or 'cost of living'), of the change in the value of the pound in relation to other currencies and, finally, a series of indices published by the Department of Trade and Industry (DTI) covering the replacement cost of a reasonable range of assets.

The question which must be answered before an index number is used for the revalorization of assets is: for what purpose is the revalorization being undertaken? If it is to calculate the cost of replacing the assets, then those index numbers compiled by the DTI would appear to be most applicable; if it is to discount the falling value of money in terms of purchasing power, then one of the other indices might apply. But the object for present purposes is to ascertain a sound base for the calculation of a profit target, and it has been argued that such a base must be the capital value of the earning power of the assets involved. None of the indices mentioned above apparently fulfils this requirement, although some may well be suitable for other purposes. Even if they were suitable they are reflections of past trends compiled from weighted samples of activity; what we are seeking is a means of placing a value on likely future events.

The more popular method of revaluation simply means commissioning professional valuers to place a value on the assets, not for the purposes of resale but on a so-called 'going concern' basis, or their worth to the business. There is no question that such a valuation involves very great professional skill and experience and a thorough knowledge of the particular business, but fundamentally it must result in a somewhat subjective assessment. The expense is, incidentally, formidable and such a revaluation of all the assets is not normally carried out more than once every five years. In spite of its imperfections, such a revaluation may be nearer the principle of ascertaining the potential earning value of the assets than the use of an index which cannot possibly give weight to the circumstances and prospects of a particular company or of the industry of which it forms part.

For a small business the expense and effort involved either in revalorization or revaluation may not be considered justified. Even in such a case it is, however, important that the management and owners shall be under no major illusion as to the earning power of the assets and hence of the profit which the business ought to achieve in the long term; and a distinct illusion can be created by relating profitability, either actual or anticipated, to the capital employed in terms of original cost. A simple device is to apply to the owners' equity (issued ordinary shares and reserves, including the balance on the profit and loss account) an index number representing the fall in the value of money year by year, such as the cost of living index published by the DTI. This method will not specifically cover changes in the earning poten-

		Original cost	Grossed up values
Year 1	Original capital	£10,000+4%	£10,400
	Profit retained	500	500
Year 2		£10,500	£10,900
	Add: 4%		436
	Profit retained	525	525
Year 3		£11,025	£11,861
	Add: 4%		474
	Profit retained	550	550
Year 4		£11,575	£12,885
	Add: 4%		515
	Profit retained	575	575
Year 5		£12,150	£13,975
	Add: 4%		559
	Profit retained	610	610
		£12,760	£15,144

tial of individual assets but it will at least produce a figure of capital employed as a basis for calculating required profits which will offset the fall in the purchasing power of money.

Consider the foregoing example which assumes a fall in the purchasing power of money continuing at 4% per annum.

The simple calculation opposite does give an indication of the false picture presented of the capital employed, and hence of the profit required, over the comparatively short period of five years and with inflation at only 4%. In the course of time the retained profit, which in the foregoing example has been calculated at approximately 5% of the equity in terms of original cost, will soon be less than the inflation cost and the business will be losing capital in real terms unless retentions are increased.

The profit target – capital structure

The forward plan must have a sound financial base and to a large extent this base will consist of the capital structure of the company. By capital structure we refer to the various funds from which finance has been obtained in the past, these funds being the different classes of share capital, reserves and loan capital, as set out on the balance sheet. For many companies, especially the smaller category, bank loans and overdrafts are, although subject to reduction at short notice, in fact held for long periods and if so may well be considered as part of the capital structure for present purposes. In any event the availability of further finance, for instance by means of an overdraft facility, is an important aspect of the financial base.

The nature and pattern of the capital structure, especially the extent to which fixed interest is payable on loans and preference shares, is a significant factor in the calculation of the profit target; it will also influence the means by which further funds can be obtained. For example, a company which has a heavy burden of fixed-interest capital may have difficulty in obtaining further risk capital; and a company with a low issued capital in ordinary shares, but perhaps high reserves, could be a questionable vehicle for the suppliers of loan capital because of the small commitment by the risk bearers.

It is not the function of this book to examine the technical intricacies involved in the provision of finance, from the money markets or otherwise, but the purpose of this section is to indicate some of the major factors in relation to capital structure which will affect the planning and performance of the company.

The essential requirement is that the capital structure should be appropriate to the operational needs of the business; and it may have to be adapted to meet these needs. It is important to observe that operational plans should not be unnecessarily constrained by an outdated capital structure, although this is sometimes a counsel of perfection, especially for a company which is struggling for survival. Nevertheless, the principle is that the financial function should serve and not dictate the development of the business.

As a generalization it may be said that a business needs four kinds of finance: permanent (so far as anything is permanent in a changing world); medium term, i.e. repayable in say five to twenty years; short term, generally under five years; and contingency finance. The permanent finance, to fund the hard core of the business when it is originally established, or to fund a permanent enlargement of the business, normally consists of ordinary shares or *equity*. The equity may be increased in two ways: either by an issue of further shares, or by placing some of the available profits to reserve which it is not intended to distribute by way of dividends or otherwise. A bonus issue, i.e. an issue of further shares out of reserves, is simply a formal recognition that the reserves so capitalized have become part of the permanent capital of the company. No funds are obtained by the issue of bonus shares (unless accompanied by a further issue for cash) but, in effect, the company obtained further funds when the profits which were transferred to reserve were originally made. Further equity capital should be obtained only to finance a major and long-term expansion of the business, and it is important that no more money shall be obtained from ordinary shares than is necessary for long-term requirements, otherwise the rate of dividend per share will tend to be reduced and the market value of the shares weakened. A fall in the market value of the shares will deter further investors and a fall below their nominal value will necessitate a formal write-down of the nominal value before further shares can be issued. Ordinary shares cannot be repaid save in exceptional circumstances and by application to the court.

Medium-term requirements are normally derived by issue of redeemable capital, e.g. redeemable debentures or preference shares. The issue of preference shares (which have priority of dividend over ordinary shares up to a fixed percentage) is nowadays unpopular largely because the interest is not allowable for tax purposes, as is the case with loan capital interest. Another disadvantage of preference shares is that they can only be redeemed out of profits, accumulated into a reserve equal to their redemption value, or out of a fresh issue of shares. This statutory requirement follows the legal principle that share capital cannot be reduced, save in exceptional circumstances. In consequence of the disadvantages of preference shares, medium-term capital is usually obtained in the form of loan capital, such as debentures, which may or may not be secured on the landed property of the company or on its whole undertaking.

So far as short-term finance is concerned, the most common form is by means of bank accommodation, fixed loan for the longer term and an overdraft facility for the shorter term. Many other sources of short-term finance include bills of exchange or notes payable, leasing of assets and factoring of invoices. A large volume of finance is obtained by subsidiary companies from the holding company of the group.

The distinction between short-term finance and what has been referred to above as 'contingency finance' is somewhat fine. Short-term finance indicates money which is actually raised from the various sources available. Contingency finance denotes rather the potential to raise money at short notice to meet the unexpected contingency or crisis, both of which are endemic in business. Prudent financial planning should always calculate the extent to which money can be raised by the business in a hurry. A useful source for this kind of finance is the unused overdraft facility or at least the known availability of an overdraft, and another is the existence of bills receivable which can be discounted. The negotiation of extended credit from suppliers, and the more questionable practice of simply delaying payment, are often used to conserve funds, especially by those companies with large buying power on which suppliers depend. The temporary restriction or postponement of dividends is perhaps a more creditable means of dealing with a cash crisis, for the consequent hardship is, so to speak, 'within the family'.

Because of the rapidly changing business environment most businesses need a considerable degree of flexibility in their requirements for funds. This is particularly so if the business operates in a market which is susceptible to large and especially short-term fluctuations in demand. The most carefully researched planning can be upset by the unexpected. It is for this reason that the availability of short-term finance becomes of paramount importance in the planning process. Medium-term finance is required for a programme of development which is not expected to produce a positive cash inflow until after some years. Further flexibility is imparted to medium-term finance by arranging for redemption over a period of years commencing at the appropriate future date. If the development creates a permanent expansion of the company it is usually possible to convert medium-term into permanent finance. In some cases a programme of development aimed at permanent enlargement of a company is financed by debentures which carry an option to convert into ordinary shares after a suitable period. This device has the merit of limiting the interest payable during the development period, and can be attractive to investors.

A form of capital structure which has satisfied past needs, or was merely the result of historical accident, may not be adequate in relation to future plans and may have to be reorganized. Consider the following simplified example of the capital structure of a company about to embark on a forward plan consisting of:

(a) the launching of a new product line expected to produce a positive cash inflow in ten years; and
(b) a policy of permanent expansion through acquisitions and mergers.

Present capital structure

2,000,000 ordinary shares of £1, of which 50p is paid up	£1,000,000
Free reserves	3,500,000
12½% debenture stock, redeemable in 5 years	4,000,000
	£8,500,000

The points for consideration are as follows:

1 The gearing is high, i.e. the company has a contractual liability to pay £500,000 a year (gross of tax) in interest on the debentures, thus to that extent restricting cash available as dividend to shareholders and for development. But it should be borne in mind that the interest is chargeable against profits for tax purposes and, assuming a tax rate of 50%, the net charge on the company is only 6.25%. Depending on current rates of interest, the debentures may represent cheap capital and thus justify retention, at least in part.

2 Unless some arrangement is made with the debenture holders, the £4,000,000 is due to be repaid in five years' time. Meanwhile it is desirable that a proportion of the debentures be repaid immediately to reduce the high gearing. If the debentures holders cannot obtain better terms elsewhere they would only agree to repayment before the due term if they received some compensation, for instance a premium on redemption or perhaps a favourable offer of conversion to ordinary shares. If it is desired to retain a proportion of the debentures after five years, the debenture holders would again claim compensation unless the present rate of interest was considered favourable to them.

3 Assume that the decision is to obtain the agreement of the debenture holders to an immediate repayment of £2 million and that a further £2 million is required to increase the permanent capital of the company. Of the total funds required £1 million could easily be obtained by calling up the uncalled capital of 50p a share. Probably the best way of obtaining the balance of £3 million would be by way of rights issue to the existing ordinary shareholders if they could be offered terms which would make it

uneconomic for them to refuse to subscribe. Such terms could well be the issue of a certain number of bonus shares out of the ample reserves for each additional share subscribed for in cash.

4 The analysis of the terms to be offered to shareholders in such a situation is the subject of specialized studies. For present purposes it may be sufficient to indicate that the many complex factors involved would include the following: share price; expectation of future yield and capital appreciation; current and expected market rates of return; the nature of the shareholder groups. In essence the offer would be evaluated by the shareholder (if he is properly advised) on the basis of comparative future income, irrespective of historical cost.

5 Assuming that the operations outlined above were successfully accomplished (and eliminating all complexities, such as any share premiums or debenture premiums) the new capital structure would appear as follows:

Revised capital structure

8,000,000 ordinary shares of £1 fully paid	£8,000,000
Reserves (after capitalization of £3,000,000)	500,000
Debentures (£2,000,000 having been repaid)	2,000,000
	£10,500,000

Cash obtained

Call-up of 50p a share	£1,000,000
Rights issue	3,000,000
	£4,000,000
Less: Debentures repaid (assume at par)	2,000,000
	£2,000,000

The profit target – other factors

The foregoing discussion seeks to place the assessment of a profit target for an individual company on a reasonably scientific basis. In practice, many other factors will be involved in the assessment, particularly for short-term purposes. One such factor of great practical importance is dividend policy or the policy regarding the accumulation of reserves, which is really the converse of dividend policy. This, of course, assumes that a policy has been formulated with regard to the payment of dividends and/or the retention of funds within the business. Policy in this connection means such matters as the proportion of available profit which it is decided ought to be paid out to the shareholders, as this is affected by the need to retain funds for development or to improve liquidity. Such matters are described as essentially of a short-term nature because they are bound to be influenced by external changes in, for example, national economic policies, and by internal needs such as the demands of a programme of automation or other forms of investment.

It is generally understood that dividends on ordinary shares vary in relation to profits but the larger companies tend to stabilize rates of dividend. This means that a company will be reluctant to reduce its normal rate of dividend, even though a temporary recession in profitability is being encountered. Past rates of dividend will, therefore, inevitably affect the computation of the profit target. Another very practical influence is the need to maintain profit and dividends when a further issue of capital is contemplated, because profitability has the major influence on share prices and the existence of a low price for existing shares might jeopardize the success of a further issue.

A further factor which may affect a straight arithmetical computation of the profit target as a percentage of capital employed is the existence of a substantial bank overdraft. Whilst bank accommodation is normally regarded as essentially of a short-term nature it is a fact that many companies have been able to secure funds from banks for periods extending over many years. Whether this is sound financial policy is another question. If this is the situation it is suggested that in computing capital employed for the purpose of setting up a profit target it is proper to include the bank accommodation, or at least the semi-permanent element of it.

In considering the various factors which influence the establishment of the profit target, it is relevant to consider the nature of the 'profit' which forms the subject matter of the discussion.

In the first place this must be a profit before taxation (a) because taxation is of the nature of the share of profit which is payable to the state, (b) because the rate of tax and sometimes even the method of assessment is outside the control of the management and incapable of prediction other than by guesswork and (c) because in many cases the profit calculated in accordance with normal accounting conventions bears little resemblance to profit calculated in accordance with taxation rules and practices.

Secondly, the profit under consideration is the figure *before* charging interest on preference shares or debentures, and also before charging bank interest if, as discussed above, the bank overdraft is to be considered as an element of capital employed.

Thirdly, the profit concerned is that before bringing into account so-called 'capital profits or losses' and exceptional charges or exceptional income. Capital profits or losses denote the book surplus or deficiency which arises on the disposal of a fixed asset such as an item of plant. If the proceeds of selling a fixed asset exceed the written-down value in the books (cost less accumulated depreciation) the surplus does not represent profit derived from the operations of the current period of account, but merely excessive depreciation charged in prior periods of account. Likewise if a 'loss' occurs on the disposal of plant this loss means that the depreciation charged in prior periods was inadequate. Capital profits and losses arising on wasting assets are, in essence, adjustments of profit for previous periods. Exceptional items might include unforeseeable bad debts, exchange losses and profits, defalcations and uninsured losses resulting from fire, accident or crime.

In summary, the importance must be emphasized of formulating a soundly based profit target as an essential long-term company objective which will bind together the efforts of the various managers and groups. The principles on which the calculation should be based have been discussed; likewise the fact that, like so many management tools, the calculations will inevitably be affected by circumstances, and by matters of judgement and opinion. The important matter is for an objective to be established; it can be amended if circumstances change and as experience dictates.

Specimen calculation of a profit target

Assume that the last and recent balance sheet of a business contains the following summarized figures. Assume also that the historical cost figures recorded in the accounting records have been converted by one or other of the methods previously outlined, into current values.

XYZ Group
Balance sheet

	Historical costs	*Current values*
Capital employed		
Issued capital		
Ordinary shares	£2,000,000	£2,000,000
8½% preference shares	800,000	800,000
Total issued share capital	£2,800,000	£2,800,000
Reserves		
Share premium account	£500,000	£500,000
Reserve on revaluation of assets	—	9,750,000
Revenue reserve	3,200,000	3,200,000
Total reserves	£3,700,000	£13,450,000
Loan capital		
10% debenture stock	£500,000	£500,000
Total capital employed	£7,000,000	£16,750,000
Employment of the capital		
Fixed assets	£5,000,000	£15,000,000
Investments	500,000	600,000
Total fixed assets and investments	£5,500,000	£15,600,000

Current assets		
Cash	£100,000	£100,000
Debtors and prepaid expenses	1,200,000	1,200,000
Stocks and work in progress	1,300,000	1,600,000
Total current assets	£2,600,000	£2,900,000
Current liabilities		
Bank overdraft	£400,000	£400,000
Creditors	1,500,000	1,500,000
Total current liabilities	£1,900,000	£1,900,000
Net current assets	£700,000	£1,000,000
Patents and trade marks	—	£150,000
Goodwill	£800,000	—
New assets	£7,000,000	£16,750,000

Notes on the above presentation:

1 The first point that will probably strike the reader is the very large surplus of current values over the figures of historical cost shown in the balance sheet. This surplus is largely represented by the current value of fixed assets, but the difference is by no means extraordinary, as many companies have found when they have undertaken a revaluation of fixed assets. It is true that the accuracy of any method of revaluation or revalorization must be subject to severe limitations, as mentioned above, but the very size of the difference indicates the necessity of making the best estimate possible of current values.

2 For the purpose of the long-term profit target, and using historical figures, the capital employed in this company is £7,000,000. On the reasonable assumption that the company ought to earn at least 10% on the capital employed, the profit target based on historical costs would be £700,000. On the basis of the revaluation of the assets, however, the capital employed is

£16,750,000 and the profit target at 10% becomes £1,675,000. The exact value of the capital in terms of current values may be subject to questions of opinion but, if this example is at all representative, it does mean that in the absence of a revaluation of the assets management may be setting their sights at far too low a level of profitability.

3 In this example the current value of the investments is shown as above the original cost; in some situations the reverse might have occurred. For the purpose of the adjustment of investment costs to current values it would be wise to use an average of recent market values, especially where the quoted value of the investments tended to fluctuate widely. Where investments do not have an ascertainable market value, the appropriate proportion of the equity acquired could be used, again subject to that equity having been adjusted to reflect current values. Such an adjustment should not be difficult to enforce where the investment was in an associate or subsidiary company but would be difficult to calculate otherwise. A possible alternative is to calculate the present value of the expected future earnings of the company concerned and to use the appropriate proportion of the resultant figure.

4 The original balance sheet figures show that the patents and trade marks have been written down to a nominal figure, as is quite customary for reasons of prudence. The problem of placing a current value on such assets is clearly difficult but a reasonable estimate of their saleable value could be made. The saleable value will then be the value forgone by retaining these assets and, accordingly, the eventual profit target will include the return which could be obtained on these assets if they were sold. Their real value to the business is the capitalized value of the profit which they are likely to bring to the business, but this is extremely difficult, if not impossible, to separate from the aggregate profit.

5 Goodwill arising on consolidation has been treated as of NIL value for the purpose of assessing a profit target. This figure would represent the excess of the cost of assets acquired over their book value in the subsidiaries' accounts, and will be incorporated in the revised valuations already placed upon the

different asset groups. There is no need to attempt an assessment of the value of real goodwill. Real goodwill may be, as a learned judge once put it, 'the probability that the old customers will resort to the old place of business', but it is more specifically the capitalized value of 'super profits', i.e. profits above a basic return. If one were able to make an assessment of goodwill in such terms, and include this in the figure of capital employed, it would mean that the business was setting itself a target to obtain super profits on the capitalized value of existing super profits which, if carried to extremes, would result in an absurdity.

6 The specimen minimum profit targets referred to in point (2) were expressed as amounts per annum and calculated on the revised total of capital employed at the beginning of the budgetary period. It has already been emphasized that the planning period for business must cover much more than a year and that the profit target, in consequence, must be a target to be achieved over a period of years, probably five as a minimum. Since most businesses retain substantial proportions of the profits they make, it is necessary for the planned retentions to be added to original capital employed at, for convenience, annual intervals. This implies a rising figure of profitability each year. In the example set out in the foregoing, and assuming that, after taxation and dividends, 20% of the profit was to be retained in the business, the profit target for the next five years would be calculated (in round figures) as on the facing page.

If some readers find that the growth indicated by the above specimen figures is small compared with the growth of many leading UK companies, it should be borne in mind that no account has been taken above of inflation. The growth shown by the monetary figures of capital employed and turnover has in most companies included a substantial inflationary element.

7 When comparing the actual profit achieved against the target set in some such manner as indicated, it is important that the 'profit' for that purpose should be regarded as the surplus *before* charging preference share interest, and before debenture interest. Bank interest should, however, be deducted from income because, in the following example, the bank overdraft has not been

	Capital employed £	Profit target @ 10% £
1 Original capital employed	16,750,000	1,675,000
Add: Profit retained 20%	335,000	
2 Capital employed	17,085,000	1,709,000
Add: Profit retained	342,000	
3 Capital employed	17,427,000	1,743,000
Add: Profit retained	349,000	
4 Capital employed	17,776,000	1,778,000
Add: Profit retained	356,000	
5 Capital employed	18,132,000	1,813,000
Add: Profit retained	363,000	
6 Capital employed	18,495,000	
Total profit required over the five years:		£8,718,000

considered to be part of the capital employed. In other words, current assets are assumed to be available for repaying the overdraft just as they are assumed to be available for paying the creditors.

3 The level of activity

Which comes first – sales or production?

Theorists will argue interminably as to whether the sales forecast or the production budget should come first. In fact, this apparent dilemma is not a real one. Later in this chapter it is explained that the logical succession of steps to be taken in the exercise of forward planning depends very largely on the circumstances in which these plans are being prepared. Such 'circumstances' include the nature of the enterprise, the present and probable future conditions affecting the particular business concerned, and the policy which the management decides to adopt for coping with the circumstances. This is not to suggest that a business should establish forward plans in a haphazard manner. On the contrary, the dominating theme of this book is that both planning and control should proceed by steps which logically follow one from the other. The fact is that every business has its own 'key' problem to face and the crux of the matter is to isolate that problem and to give it priority of importance in the budgetary processes. Whatever that key factor may be the sales forecast needs to be prepared first, if only to provide a yardstick by which the key factor can be measured. Thus, whilst in a particular business the production budget may be of primary importance, the sales forecast must first be prepared in order to determine the necessary factory loading and output. In other words, the real question is not which comes first – sales or production – but which is of primary importance.

Businesses are often described as either 'marketing orientated' or 'production orientated'. The expression *marketing orientated* appears to apply to those concerns where the greater part of the aggregate management effort is spent on marketing problems, such as those in the highly competitive consumer products field. The reason for this concentration on marketing is that management believes that the key factor for success lies in solving marketing problems first; this is akin to what Mary Parker Follett refers to as 'the law of the situation'. Marketing-orientated companies are those where the direction of all functions can be quickly and effectively adapted to changes in demand. In such cases it follows that, after establishing the desirable limits of profit in relation to capital, the next item to consider both in terms of importance and timing is the preparation of the sales forecast.

Typical *production-orientated* businesses are those whose success depends more on the technical competence of the product, where the volume and profitability of sales is less influenced by advertising and selling techniques *per se.* The kind of businesses which are frequently described thus are those of an industrial engineering nature and those which carry out substantial work for government departments. Although in such cases the sales forecast will still need to be prepared first, the production budget will be of primary importance.

Nevertheless, the attempt to place businesses into one or other of the above two categories produces many anomalies and can be shown to be a gross oversimplification of the nature of business. Much depends, for example, on the level of demand in relation to the capacity of the business. Thus, where a company producing consumer products is finding difficulty in meeting the demand, the direction of the major planning effort should be to find ways of increasing output. Conversely, where a company selling industrial products is struggling to utilize capacity to the full, the emphasis needs to be placed on selling the capacity. Whilst this may appear obvious, it needs stating if only to highlight the necessity for directing the thinking and efforts of management towards the problems of greatest importance.

What management seeks is the correct balance between the selling effort and the producing effort. At a particular point of time in any business, whether marketing or production orientated, there will generally be one key problem to be overcome in achieving a desirable level of profit. The secret lies in isolating that problem. In some companies the key factor may be overcapacity in relation to demand. In electronics the key factor is frequently the effectiveness or otherwise of the research and development function. In particular companies the factor may be the supply of key personnel, or of an essential but not necessarily expensive item of material. In each case the key factor in the situation will limit the entire activities of the business, and in costing terminology this is otherwise referred to as the *limiting factor*.

The principle of basing the whole of the budgetary process on the consideration of the limiting factor in the situation avoids the problem of deciding whether the business is marketing or production orientated, and is particularly applicable to the planning of service industries which do not readily fall into either of these two categories. Thus, in a retail store the limiting factor is often the counter space that can be made available; in an airline it may be the frequency of engine changes; for a professional man it could be the ability to play golf!

The supply of cash will always be a limiting factor and may be decisive in a period of credit squeeze. Nevertheless, in more normal times – or, put more bluntly, in the interval between financial crises – it is not especially difficult to obtain funds for a promising enterprise.

The discussion so far concerns an established enterprise. When an entirely new enterprise is considered the whole approach to the budgetary procedure is much clearer. By a new enterprise, is contemplated not only the setting up of a company to exploit an idea or invention, but also a project for developing a new line of sales in an existing company. In such circumstances the first thing to do is to assess the size of the potential market and to produce a sales forecast. Clearly, it would be dangerous and foolhardy to set up an enterprise without knowing whether it is likely to be too large or too small for the purpose in mind.

So far this chapter has emphasized and attempted to illustrate the fact that the sales forecast is by no means always the most important aspect of budgetary procedures. But because it enables the limiting factor, whatever it may be, to be seen in its proper perspective, it is the sales forecast which needs to be prepared first.

The size of the potential market

The modern technique of market research represents a complete study on its own. It is nevertheless of essential importance that the findings of market research be integrated into financial planning. Market research can be expensive and is justified, at least according to the philosophy running through this book, only if it is designed to give the business more profit than it would otherwise obtain. The general purpose of market research is to analyse the nature of demand, but its more immediate purpose is to quantify what a business could sell over a particular period of time and within a particular geographical area. The time period and the geographical area are matters of management objective and policy which, as stated above, are the two prime prerequisites of forward planning. In ascertaining what a particular business could sell it is logical first to assess the size of the whole market for a particular line and then to decide what share of that market the business can feasibly obtain. The assessment of the total market potential needs to be reduced to precise figures, or at least to upper and lower limits. The market share to be aimed at by the business will depend on a consideration of many circumstances, such as the potential competition, the capacity of the business and the intentions of the management.

Because the ultimate results of a business, particularly the profit, are expressed in the universal medium of money, the potential sales must also be expressed in monetary terms. In a sense, therefore, the sales forecast, which will issue from market research, is closely bound up with the question of the right price. The right price and the economic volume of output are problems susceptible to financial measurements and accordingly must be dictated by financial considerations. The logical conclusion is that market research, at least in the sense of ascertaining the market potential, is a vital element in financial planning and control. It is unfortunate that in some businesses the accountant takes little part in this important preliminary exercise in forward planning.

Given that financial planning is substantially long-term planning, then it follows that market research cannot end at an assessment of the present market potential for a product or service. In a world where industrialization is growing rapidly in both old and new nations, two changes in particular can occur in the present market available to a business; the first is that the total market may well increase, and the second is that the share of the market obtainable by one company may tend to decrease as competition intensifies. These two trends are especially noticeable with products which fill a real consumer need, such as heavy vehicles produced in the UK in the context of the world market. On the other hand there are many examples of declining markets, often due to the appearance of substitutes, such as occurred when artificial fibres caused a steady decline in the market for natural fibres. Although in some areas the findings of market research are by no means certain, it is nevertheless important that the *trend* of the total market potential and of the likely market share should be assessed.

If some reasonable, objective form of market research is not carried out, the sales managers in preparing their forecasts can have recourse only to the trend of past sales, supplemented by intuition or 'flair', which appear to be a much valued, if somewhat mysterious, attribute of the sales executive. However, reliance on past sales may be more dangerous than flair. The frequently used device of adding a percentage to last year's turnover is really little more than a self-defeating form of incentive and is certainly not a sound basis for planning the intricate affairs of a business. At the risk of undue repetition, it should be emphasized that planning means looking ahead; not looking behind. And the justification for looking ahead is that in a rapidly changing world the future path may bear little resemblance to the past one. If a business aims simply to achieve a certain percentage increase on past sales it has implied no idea of what level or mix of sales it is capable of obtaining. Unfortunately UK industry is littered with erstwhile great names which are now struggling for existence because they have been overtaken by foreign competitors. In some cases – the Japanese, for example – successful foreign competitors had no great industrial past to look back upon.

Assessing potential sales

We have suggested that the logical approach to the preparation of a sales forecast is to begin with an objective analysis of the market with a view to quantifying the market potential over the planning period. A great deal of statistical information is available for this purpose, such as the DTI *Monthly and Annual*

Digest of Statistics, information collected by trade associations and by market research agencies. Where a consumer product is involved, figures are available on the population by areas of the country, of the homes and age groups; if an industrial product is being produced it is often possible to obtain, either from published data or from government departments, information as to the industries likely to buy the product; in the case of components or accessories, detailed figures are often available on the production of the product of which the accessory or component will form part.

It would be foolish for a business to ignore the wealth of information available for the purposes in mind; but, at the same time, businessmen are only too well aware that success in forecasting is not a matter of statistics alone. Nor does it end with the application of sophisticated mathematical techniques to the statistics. Management has to apply to the statistics qualities of judgement which cannot be expressed in numerical terms; the factors, internal and external to the business, are innumerable. And having weighed the factors as best it can, management then sets out a forecast which is less a statement of probabilities than an expression of intentions, targets to be reached, whatever the difficulties likely to be encountered on the way.

As some indication of the matters of judgement involved in preparing a forecast of potential sales in an apparently simple situation, we set out below the elements of a purely fictitious, but in many respects realistic, case.

One of the key industries in this country is the motorcar industry; it also happens to be one for which precise and regular statistics of production and vehicle registrations are available. Assume, therefore, that an enterprise is about to be established to produce and market some gadget for fitment on private motorcars. Assume, too, that there are at present ten million private cars on the roads in this country and that it is estimated that production for home sales will rise from one million in the present year by 100,000 a year. The first question the investigator must decide is what proportion of existing car owners are likely to buy the gadget in the next year and in subsequent years. The next question is what proportion of the new cars sold are likely to be fitted with the gadget. When these questions have been decided, probably by the expertise of the market research specialist, consideration must be given to the time when competition may be expected and the share of the market likely to remain with the innovators. However expert and precise the result of market research, the last question is one for which there will be few facts or even hints to guide the decision. Certainly the experience of people who have launched similar products in similar situations would be valuable, assuming it is obtainable. By whatever processes they are arrived at, let us assume that in the end the following figures are finally agreed as an acceptable forecast of potential sales by the organization concerned.

Year	*New car production*	*% of new cars*	*New cars*	*Existing cars*	*Potential market*	*Share of market*	*Potential sales*
1	1000.0	1%	10.0	9.0	19.0	100%	19.0
2	1100.0	3%	33.0	5.0	38.0	90%	34.0
3	1300.0	5%	65.0	5.0	70.0	80%	56.0
4	1500.0	5%	75.0	5.0	80.0	70%	56.0
5	1700.0	5%	85.0	6.0	91.0	70%	63.7

(Figures are in thousands)

Clearly, the final forecasts represent little more than intelligent guesses based on the best evidence available. The point is that they do set targets which are practical possibilities. In about the third year, when experience has been obtained of actual demand and competition, it will be possible to amend the estimates on a more realistic basis and to carry them forward for a further number of years. But meanwhile the risk element is high and the aimed profitability must likewise be high to offset the risk.

Isolating the limiting factor

The next exercise is to consider the extent to which this sales forecast can be met by the facilities which are available or which can be made available. Normally, this is a question of comparing potential sales with potential production capacity, but production capacity may vary from time to time because it will depend upon the availability of a number of factors – materials, labour, space, plant and finance. If it is found that production capacity exceeds sales requirements, then it will be the market itself which is the limiting factor. In the situation under consideration, however, it is a question of bringing into being resources adequate to meet the estimated demand. It would be foolish and time-wasting to proceed with the detailed budgeting process until management has ascertained the single factor which was likely to limit the output. Once that factor has been isolated, management is faced with a simple alternative; either (a) to accept the limitation imposed on activity or (b) to seek ways of overcoming the limitation. If, for example, the limiting factor is found to be the supply of a particular component, then consideration might be given to altering the design or finding a substitute. If the limitation is space or plant, this might be overcome by subcontracting part of the work.

Frequently the limiting factor is the number of operatives that can be accommodated in the premises available. The number of operatives will determine the man hours that can be applied to the work; subject, of course, to overtime and shift work, which is normally expensive and difficult to organize. Assume in the situation under consideration that no particular problems are foreseen regarding the provision of finance, the availability of machinery or the supply of materials, and that the overall limitation is the number of direct man hours that can be generated in the factory premises available. If a number of separate operations are involved in producing the product, the problem can be narrowed still further by isolating the key operation and the number of man hours that can be applied to that operation. For simplicity, assume that in the present case a single assembly operation is involved and the direct man hours which can be produced are assessed as follows:

Space available for	100 direct operatives
On the basis of 49 working weeks in a year and 36 effective direct hours per week (allowing for paid sickness and inevitable idle time) this gives potential direct hours of: 100×49×36	= 176,400 hours per annum

It is now necessary to convert the sales forecast into units of the limiting factor – man hours of work involved – and thus to compare the potential sales with the potential capacity. Assuming that, as a result of an exercise in work study, it is estimated that each unit involves three man hours of work, then it is apparent that the production facilities are capable of producing

$$\frac{176{,}400}{3} = 58{,}800 \text{ units per annum}$$

It will be observed from the sales forecast that this capacity is slightly more than adequate to meet sales requirements in the third and fourth year, but that there will be underutilization of capacity in the first and second years and insufficient capacity in the fifth year.

The situation is not, however, quite so simple as expressed here because (a) the sales forecast does not represent actual deliveries, and (b) no account has yet been taken of desirable stock levels. Nevertheless, it seems reasonably certain that management has a problem so far as the early and later years are concerned, because underutilization of capacity usually means loss and insufficient capacity means profits forgone. Reconciliation of sales and production activities in the first year will need particularly detailed study, as much will depend on the speed with which the optimum level of output can be built up, and on the growth of the order intake. For the moment, however, the broader and longer-term problem is being considered; for this must be solved first if the business is to avoid operating on a hand to mouth basis.

The next exercise is to convert the sales forecast, which represents orders to be received, into deliveries to the customers. The allowable delay between receipt of an order and delivery to the customer is largely a matter of marketing policy, but it is relevant to observe, in passing, that one of the easiest ways of losing customer goodwill is the failure to meet delivery dates. The implementation of delivery dates depends entirely on achieving the right accord between the production and the selling function, and this must begin at the planning stage.

Suppose that one month's delay is acceptable between receipt of order and delivery. The forecast of orders is now converted into a forecast of deliveries required, in the manner shown in the next example.

Forecasting production and stocks

It is now necessary to determine required levels of finished stocks. This is a decision which can be guided by constructing a

Year	In thousands of units Orders receivable	Deliveries
1	19.0	
Less: $\frac{1}{12}$th	1.6	
		17.4
2	34.0	
Less: $\frac{1}{12}$th	2.8	
	31.2	
Add: from year 1	1.6	
		32.8
3	56.0	
Less: $\frac{1}{12}$th	4.7	
	51.3	
Add: from year 2	2.8	
		54.1
4	56.0	
Less: $\frac{1}{12}$th	4.7	
	51.3	
Add: from year 3	4.7	
		56.0
5	63.7	
Less: $\frac{1}{12}$th	5.3	
	58.4	
Add: from year 4	4.7	
		63.1

mathematical model of the various factors involved. For present purposes, however, it may be sufficient to mention that the main considerations are as follows:

1 The time lag between completion in the production workshops, including inspection, and the availability of the product for delivery. The operations involved are physical transport to stores, paperwork, storing in racks, transfer to goods-outwards department packing, and making arrangements for transportation. This time lag is often ignored in assessing stock levels, but it does mean that during this period the company is holding a certain volume of stock. It is important to reduce the time lag because stock is idle capital and means not only loss of interest on the capital involved, but also administrative cost actually being incurred.

2 The size of customer orders. Some kind of average or medium size will have to be calculated. There is a level beyond which it is uneconomic to hold large stocks merely for the purpose of meeting promptly the exceptional large order. On the other hand, if the stocks are not held at an adequate level there is a danger that many customers' orders will be delayed whilst the requirements for one or more large orders are being met.

3 (i) Cost of space (rent or interest on capital), maintenance and building occupation costs generally.
 (ii) Administrative costs, including salaries of storekeepers and clerks, depreciation and maintenance of equipment, insurance.
 (iii) Deterioration of stock.
 (iv) Interest on the investment in the stocks.

In addition to the above costs it may be possible to assess the cost of failing to hold adequate stocks, i.e. the cost of lost sales. In this, as in most planning exercises, the first step is to find the key factor in the situation.

Frequently, the first key factor to be considered is the probable delay between the completion of the product in the works and dispatch to the customer. A delay of some duration is inevitable to deal with the physical handling of the product in the works, the recording into and out of stores, and arranging for transport to the customer. So far as the last factor is concerned, clearly long-distance and overseas transportation must be considered separately. Assume, for the purposes of the example, that the normal delay is assessed at two weeks, then, if the delivery time of one month after receipt of order is to be met, production must always be at least two weeks in advance of the deliveries required.

The second factor for consideration is the normal expected size of customer orders. Information may be obtained from market research and in many cases customers so that the product may be grouped by average size of order. Thus, direct sales to the ultimate consumer are likely to be in units, but wholesalers and large purchasers may order many units at a time. It thus becomes necessary to ensure, within the limits of reasonably economic stockholding quantities, that sufficient stock is carried to meet the large orders, which will almost certainly be the most economical to satisfy.

In order to illustrate the foregoing argument, the following simplified calculations are shown:

1st year

Customer categories	A	B	C	Total
Average units per order	5	10	50	
Orders per annum	1,600	500	88	
Therefore: units per annum	8,000	5,000	4,400	17,400
Average orders per week (50-week year)	32	10	1.76	

Because of the desirability of promptly meeting orders from the valuable 'C' category of customer, it is estimated that up to three orders may be received from this category in any one week. In this case the stockholding levels must be calculated on the basis of:

	A	B	C	Total
(Orders)	32	10	3	
In two weeks the figures become:	64	20	6	
Multiply by numbers of units:	5	10	50	
Gives stocks required in units:	320	200	300	820

If the numbers of orders, or quantity per order, were likely to change, a fresh calculation of this nature would be required each year. Assume, however, that the pattern is not expected to change, then the percentage of stock to deliveries in the first year (4.7%) may be applied to later years. Production requirements may now be calculated as shown below.

		In thousands of units	
Year 1			
	Deliveries	17.4	
Add:	Stock required	0.8	
	Output required		18.2
Year 2			
	Deliveries	32.8	
Less:	Starting stock	0.8	
		32.0	
Add:	Stock required	1.5	
	Output required		33.5
Year 3			
	Deliveries	54.1	
Less:	Starting stock	1.5	
		52.6	
Add:	Stock required	2.5	
	Output required		55.1
Year 4			
	Deliveries	56.0	
Less:	Starting stock	2.5	
		53.5	
Add:	Stock required	2.6	
	Output required		56.1
Year 5			
	Deliveries	63.1	
Less:	Starting stock	2.6	
		60.5	
Add:	Stock required	3.0	
	Output required		63.5

The probable financial effects of the plan

So far the potential market, the likely share of the market, the orders receivable, the deliveries, production and stocks required have been assessed – all in units of product. It is necessary now to apply monetary values to the figures to obtain a broad appreciation (subject to more detailed budgeting) of the extent to which the anticipated activity is likely to achieve the required profit. It will also be necessary to check whether the finance available is adequate for the purposes.

It is clear, from the figures produced so far, that production will not utilize capacity until some time after the fourth year, and that there is then a problem of normal capacity being inadequate to meet sales requirements. The problems of underutilization of capacity in the early years and of inadequate capacity in the fifth year will need special consideration, but it is no use proceeding further with the skeleton plan constructed so far until the business is assured of making an adequate profit, and will be able to finance operations when working at or about capacity. The fourth year looks near enough to capacity working to be used for the test.

The exercise of calculating expected profitability falls naturally under two headings: *income* and *expenditure*, or 'sales' and 'costs'. The only element to be introduced for the purpose of calculating the sales figures in monentary terms is the price. The costs are best considered under the following four distinct headings:

1 Making the product.
2 Selling and distributing the product.
3 Administering the business.
4 Financing the business.

Within the cost headings it will be useful to distinguish between those expenses which vary in relation to the activity and those which are relatively static or 'fixed'. The conventional classification of expense into the *fixed* and *variable* is of necessity a very rough apportionment, for all expenses must be made variable in relation to activity in the long run. The real point is that some items of expenditure take longer to alter than others. However, when considering the effect on profits of activity below or greater than capacity working, the distinction between which expenses are likely to alter and which will be unaffected will simplify the calculations.

There is another and more immediate advantage in segregating fixed from variable expenses for forward-planning purposes. The difference between the income (largely sales) and the variable costs, wherever they arise, is called 'the contribution' because it may be regarded as the contribution towards meeting the fixed expenses and the minimum profit required. Therefore, by assessing the fixed expenses, which cannot normally be avoided at a certain level of activity, and adding this total to the required profit, the required 'contribution' may be ascertained. It then remains a problem of finding the right balance between sales income and variable costs which will achieve this contribution and, maybe, improve on it. The approach to financial planning discussed above may be expressed in the following summarized form:

required minimum profit	=	percentage of capital employed
required profit + fixed costs	=	contribution
contribution	=	income minus variable costs

This approach may be illustrated in more specific form by its application to some specimen figures. For the purpose of presenting the broad principles involved much of the detailed assessments of costs has been ignored and, indeed, at this preliminary stage in the whole intricate exercise there is little to be gained by complicating the essential issues with unnecessary detail.

The first problem is to assess the capital which will be employed in producing around 56.1 units and selling 56.0 units, as forecast for the fourth year. Shorn of all detail, let it be assumed that the investment at this level is calculated as follows:

Working capital	£120,000
Premises	1,500,000
Plant and other fixed assets	380,000
Capital employed	£2,000,000

Assume also that the minimum profit required, having regard to risk and the return available on similar investments, is 15%. The profit target is therefore decided at:

15% of £2,000,000 =	£300,000

It is now necessary to assess the fixed costs per annum which will be necessary to sustain the level of activity planned. These fixed costs will consist largely of the rent and cost of occupying the buildings, depreciation and maintenance of plant and equipment, and unavoidable administrative expenses in production, sales, and administrative departments. Assume the assessment of these fixed costs is summarized as follows:

Estimated fixed costs and contribution

Production departments	£90,000	
Sales departments	70,000	
Administration departments	140,000	
Total fixed costs		£300,000
Add: Profit target		300,000
Contribution required		£600,000

The required contribution, as above, is to be met from the difference between income from sales and the variable costs.

The calculation of the income will depend upon the price to be charged. In a market where there is considerable elasticity of demand – that is, where demand changes noticeably in response to changes in price – it is a question of deciding on the price/volume which is likely to produce the greatest return in the long run. These and other problems of price fixing have merited a separate chapter and, for the sake of simplifying the present example, it is assumed that the price is effectively fixed by the market at £20 a unit. It is true, of course, that there is a range of prices for any product – even if in some cases the range has narrow limits – but the effectiveness of minor changes to price will probably be the subject of future experiments and investigations after the product has been launched.

In the present example it is assumed that around 56,000 units will be sold. It is permissible to round this figure up to 60,000 units for simplicity of calculation, as there must be a degree of tolerance in such estimates; in any event it should not be difficult to organize this small increase in capacity. The next step is to calculate the permissible level of variable costs as follows:

Permissible variable costs

Income – 60,000 units to be sold at £20 each	£1,200,000
Deduct the required contribution, as above	600,000
Leaving permissible variable costs	£600,000

It now remains to make detailed estimates of what the variable costs are likely to be in fact. Subject to this important exercise, the following statement shows the present state of the forecast:

Profit statement at capacity

	Sales	£1,200,000
Less:	Variable costs allowable	600,000
	Contribution	£600,000
Less:	Fixed costs assessed	300,000
	Profit target	£300,000

The variable costs will include production, direct labour and direct materials (including bought-out parts for production), variable production overheads, and the variable elements of selling and administrative costs. By and large the variable production costs will move in relation to the volume of production, either expressed in units to be produced or some overall key factor, such as man hours or machine hours. Variable selling expenses will tend to move in relation to the selling activity, possibly expressed in orders receivable, and administrative variable expenses will depend on the whole activity of the concern, and may be related to total costs, man hours or some other key measure appropriate to the particular enterprise concerned.

It will be necessary for the various functions of the business to make an assessment of their likely variable expenses and costs on the best basis available – which may be a combination of work study, experience, and a touch of flair. The real arguments begin when the assessed variable costs are greater than the permissible levels arrived at by the logical process summarized above. It then becomes a question of the management seeking additional profit by reconsidering volume, price, variable costs, fixed costs and, indeed, the capital required. The plain fact is that if the permissible level of variable cost at or near capacity working is shown, after such investigations and reappraisals of the situation, to exceed the permissible level, then it would be foolish to pursue the enterprise. This is, indeed, one of the major merits of carrying out as scientific an exercise as possible in pre-planning. For the sake of completing the present illustration it will be assumed that the managers concerned have carried out careful investigations of the variable expenses which are likely to arise when they are working at the level envisaged and that the results of these investigations are as follows:

Expected variable costs at capacity		
1 Production		
Labour: 3 hours @ £2 × 60,000 units	£360,000	
Material: 60p a unit × 60,000 units	36,000	
Overheads: at, say, 50p a man hour for 3 × 60,000 = 180,000 hours	90,000	
Total production variable costs		£486,000
2 Selling		
at 80p a unit × 60,000 units	£48,000	
3 Administration		
at 30p an hour × 180,000 hours	54,000	
Total selling and administration variable expenses		102,000
Total variable costs and expenses		£588,000

The above total of variable costs is slightly below the permissible level of £600,000 so that the business should be capable of at least achieving the required profit when working at capacity. The figures may now be set out in the form of a more conventional profit and loss account.

Estimated trading and profit and loss account at capacity

	Sales			£1,200,000
Less:	Direct costs –			
	Labour		£360,000	
	Material		36,000	
	Production overheads –			
	variable	£90,000		
	fixed	90,000		
			180,000	
	Total direct costs			576,000
	Gross profit			£624,000
Less:	Operating expenses –			
	Selling –			
	variable	£48,000		
	fixed	70,000		
	Total selling expenses		£118,000	
	Administration –			
	variable	£54,000		
	fixed	140,000		
	Total administration expenses		194,000	
	Total operating expenses			312,000
	Operating profit			£312,000

Note that the final figure above is called *operating profit* and not 'net profit' because no account has yet been taken of probable interest charges, capital profits or losses, or taxation. The profit of £312,000 represents nearly 16% on the estimated capital so that the enterprise would appear to be a viable one when a reasonable level of capacity utilization is achieved.

This then is the preliminary forecast which appears to justify the enterprise. A number of problems remain to be settled, however, and they may be summarized as follows:

1 To prepare forecasts for the earlier years and endeavour to find some means of obtaining better utilization of capacity in these years, thus making them more profitable, or reducing the losses which are likely to be incurred.
2 To consider how profitability can be increased in the fourth and subsequent years.
3 To consider whether, and the extent to which, capacity can be increased so as to cope with demand expected after the fourth year.
4 To prepare detailed cash forecasts, so as to indicate the timing and nature of the finance required.

A final problem overshadowing the whole exercise, is that of adjusting the forecasts for the estimated effect of inflation. Initially, however, it will be simplest to plan in terms of a constant value of the currency.

4 The utilization of capacity

The preceding chapter demonstrated that forward planning for a business depends, amongst other factors, on the management settling a level of activity for the enterprise as a whole. This level of activity will be dictated largely by the sales forecast, subject to whatever limiting factors may restrict the implementation of the forecast. In some situations the projected sales may be insufficient to utilize the full capacity of the business and this is the situation shown in the early years of the example already given. The obvious consequence of underutilization is that the business will be forgoing potential profit from the spare capacity. This is a frequent cause of a low return being achieved on the capital employed and is therefore a circumstance which merits the closest attention of managers. The purpose of this chapter is to examine the causes and effects of underutilization and to suggest some remedies.

It is first necessary to consider the precise implications of the expression 'underutilization of capacity'. The capacity of a business cannot be adequately defined as the potential to produce the particular goods and services which it is currently producing or has in the past been accustomed to produce. There are too many examples, especially during wartime, of factories adapting their resources to produce goods which they had never before manufactured, for this to be a satisfactory definition. Capacity may be more appropriately defined in this context as the ability of a business unit to produce work. Thus, men and women can train themselves, or be trained, to carry out many quite different kinds of operations and, to a more limited extent, machines often have the same adaptability. Limitations on the use of the business premises are comparatively few. The problem is to quantify such a wide interpretation of the word capacity.

Work involves the employment of the resources of a business, and underutilization of capacity means that the resources of a business are inadequately employed. The resources are basically the land and buildings, plant and machinery, equipment of all kinds, and the materials in stock. To this list could be added the less tangible but equally valuable resources of reputation, goodwill, expertise, and all the skills and qualities of the management and personnel. Financial planning must be concerned largely with those resources on which a more or less precise value can be placed and for such purposes it is more convenient to regard the human resources as those which enable the business to make use of its material resources with varying degrees of efficiency.

Under utilization may occur either (a) when the material resources are not being used at all for a period, e.g. in the case of idle machinery, or (b) when the resources are being used inefficiently. It would be a very efficient business indeed where all the resouces were employed in the most profitable manner all the time – in fact it would be incredible. But the job of management is to strive towards this ideal, and it is fair to state that the extent to which management is able to achieve this utopian situation is a measure of its efficiency.

From a purely monetary point of view, full and efficient utilization of capacity is tantamount to full and efficient use of the business capital. The resources are what has been acquired by the capital invested in or borrowed by the business. In this context we cannot therefore ignore cash and the other ingredients of working capital (the excess of current assets over current liabilities). Although the directors of some companies appear to take pride in the existence of a large surplus of working capital, what they fail to acknowledge is the fact that this surplus is idle capital which could and should have been earning a return. It is, of course, prudent to maintain a reserve of finance in the form of net liquid capital against unexpected calls for finance, but the amount should be severely limited.

There appear to be two major situations where underutilization of resources occurs. One such is where facilities are acquired to develop a new line of sales and it is then some years before those facilities can be fully employed. This is the situation shown in the early years of the example given in the previous chapter. Some remedies for that situation will be examined later in this chapter. The other situation is where a business has expanded its facilities over the years in relation to the growth in the demand for its products and services, and then encounters a recession in activity.

A recession may be worldwide, nationwide, applicable only to a particular industry, or simply to an individual business. In each case the job of the manager is to plan the affairs of the business in order to minimize the effects of the recession so far as that business is concerned. Since the sunspot theory of depressions has been somewhat discredited the businessman has had some difficulty in predicting when a recession in activity on a national scale will occur. He is, however, able to foresee a decline in activity peculiar to his own business by the aid of market research or the more simple expedient of watching the order intake.

Effects on costs and profits

One remedy for underutilization is to find some way of using the spare facilities in a profitable manner. What is 'profitable' in this regard will be discussed later. The other remedy is to reduce or eliminate the excess costs. Too often businessmen appear to accept the inevitability of low profits during a recession by talking glibly about 'under-recovered fixed costs'. This, we suggest, is an example of a well-worn phrase having a somewhat hypnotic influence. The implication is that there is a certain category of expense, called 'fixed costs', which is completely incapable of reduction. In fact, 'fixed costs' is only an accounting term used to denote those elements of cost that do not vary directly with sales or production. They are certainly not 'fixed' in the sense that they are immutable, because almost all costs *can* be reduced by management action. All too often the problem lies in the lack of such management action. An illusion of a different kind is created by talking about 'variable costs' as though this second category of business expense can be altered at will. The essential fact which the businessman knows from his experience is that some expenses take longer and require more decisive action to eliminate than others; and the nature of the expenses concerned depends on the nature of the business and the prevailing conditions. The two categories of cost which are pertinent to the present discussion are (a) those expenses incurred by holding facilities in being and (b) those expenses incurred by putting the facilities to work.

The cost of holding facilities in being, whether they consist of unused space, idle machinery, surplus stock, or other resources, is essentially the cost of maintenance, recording, accounting, managerial and staff time, and the interest on the capital involved. It is safe to say that the management of many an otherwise efficient business might receive some rude shocks if the cost of idle or inadequately employed facilities was assessed. The costs of using the facilities are the additional costs which will be incurred when the idle space, plant, etc., is used to produce goods or services, and these costs will include not only direct wages and direct materials but also additional indirect costs, or overheads, such as electricity and consumable stores. A further element in this analysis of the costs involved in the problem of under-utilization is the potential profit which could be earned on the capital which the unused facilities represent. For this purpose we conceive profit to be something additional to basic interest. Profit is the reward for enterprise and risk taking; interest is the payment for the use of money.

In summary: the costs associated with idle facilities may be classified under the following four headings:

(a) The costs of holding the facilities in being;
(b) Interest on the capital represented by the facilities;
(c) The costs of using the facilities;
(d) Profit forgone by failing to use the facilities.

If the foregoing analysis of the costs of idle facilities is sound, it follows that the problem of overcoming a situation of under-utilization should be considered in four stages:

1 Can all the above four categories of cost be recovered (the ideal solution)?
2 Can interest on capital but no profit be obtained in addition to the first two headings of cost?

3 Can the costs of using the facilities be recovered plus a contribution towards paying the costs of holding them in being?

4 Can the costs of holding the facilities in being be reduced?

These questions are discussed below.

Question 1 Can the idle facilities be used to produce income which will cover all costs and provide a reasonable profit?

In normal circumstances, it is unlikely that this question will be answered in the affirmative because if it can be so answered the facilities would hardly have been idle in the first place. There may, however, be occasions when concentration by management on standard products has prevented attention being given to other uses of the plant for profitable purposes, in other words diversification of the product line. The dangers are that in using the idle facilities for a new product the eventual development of the main product may be prejudiced. The decision must be based on the answer to the question as to which course of action is likely to produce the greatest long-term profitability. Clearly the merits of diversification as a means of spreading the risk would influence such a decision; but so might wider considerations of policy such as the maintenance of the 'company image' in a particular field.

If, as is probable, there appears to be no profitable use of the surplus facilities, then management should consider the next question.

Question 2 Can the facilities be applied in a manner which will recover all costs plus only minimum interest on capital?

This question brings us to the important point that, in dealing with the problem of underutilization, it is desirable that the capital represented by the idle facilities should be quantified, in order that the minimum rate of interest thereon can be calculated. This calculation is bound to be somewhat approximate but a reasonable approximation is a better guide to decision-making than a guess. If the freehold of the premises is owned a simple calculation on the basis of relative floor area should produce a reasonable valuation of the unoccupied space:

Value of premises		£1,500,000
Surplus space		25,000 sq ft (10%)
Total space		250,000 sq ft
10% of £1,500,000	=	£150,000

If the basic rate of interest on capital is assumed to be 10% then the unused space is costing the company in interest: 10% of £150,000 = £15,000 pa.

Similarly, the underutilized investment in the plant can be assessed by comparing normal working hours with the expected hours the plant is likely to be used. The capital invested in the idle stocks is the money which could be obtained by selling them – perhaps a small amount, but possibly quite significant. An assessment of the working capital which has to be retained because of the existence of idle facilities is more difficult but not impossible.

It could well be that there is no possibility of obtaining even basic interest on capital by employing the unused facilities, so that management must now consider the next question.

Question 3 Can the facilities be used to produce a contribution towards the existing expenses?

'Making a contribution towards the existing expenses' means the same thing as 'providing a surplus between income and the additional expenses incurred in producing the income'. On the assumption that the existing expenses of holding the facilities in being will be incurred anyway, any such surplus will increase the sum total of the business profit. The additional expense is of the nature of the economist's marginal cost (although, in strictness, marginal cost is the theoretical cost of producing *one* more unit) and the additional income is the marginal income. Taking the long-term view it becomes a question of setting off *relevant* rather than additional expenses against additional income, on the grounds that the existing cost of facilities retained to produce the income could have been eliminated or applied to the purpose of earning income in another direction. Thus, even if the unused facilities can be employed in earning income which covers only additional cost, the validity of operating in this manner depends upon the period of time involved in relation to the time which will occur before the existing costs can be eliminated. It would be unwise to eliminate facilities which are required for profit-earning activity in the near future.

Assume that the existing cost of idle facilities is:	£100,000 pa
The facilities can be employed to earn income of:	600,000 pa
At an additional cost of:	580,000 pa
Giving a 'contribution' of:	£20,000 pa

Although the total costs of the resources applied in earning the income of £600,000 amount to £100,000 + £580,000 = £680,000 it will be worth while to use the facilities in this way for by so doing overall profit of the business will be increased by £20,000 pa.

Now assume that in, say, three years the existing cost of the idle facilities could have been reduced by £60,000 pa, then it would be foolish to continue making sales at the margin shown above, because the position would become:

	Income		£600,000 pa
Less:	Relevant costs –		
	Additional costs	£580,000	
	Existing costs which could have been saved	60,000	
			640,000
	Loss		£(40,000)

The foregoing argument leads into the fourth and final question.

Question 4 Can the existing costs be reduced?

This, it is felt, is the last resource in a situation of under-utilization. It would be the only line of approach left where there was no possibility of using the facilities even for the purpose of making a 'contribution'. As indicated above, the elimination of the cost of idle facilities would be applicable where the savings to be achieved exceeded any contribution which could be produced by using the facilities. During a temporary recession, or whilst a product or service was under development, the savings to be achieved by eliminating these costs would need to be balanced against the cost of re-establishing the resources in equipment, material, and manpower which the costs represented.

The circumstances where it would be essential to reduce the cost of idle facilities are those where there was no reasonable prospect of ever using them in a remunerative manner; this should be recognized without delay and action will need to be taken to cut the cost of the idle resources quickly and drastically. This will mean disposing of redundant plant, materials, and personnel, even if, in the case of the first two categories, a *book loss* results. The disposal of redundant plant and materials will produce an automatic further redundancy in space, personnel and administrative systems, which can be tackled next. It might be possible to let the free space, but if it represented a very significant drain on profits, the final solution would be to move into more economic premises.

Business managers are often reluctant to dispose of surplus resources, partly because they feel a use might eventually be found for them and partly because of the book loss which is likely to be recorded in the accounts on disposal. The possibility that the idle resources might eventually be put to a remunerative use is simply a hope, not a reason for their retention, and is incompatible with the scientific approach to business decision making. The argument for retaining idle facilities would be sound enough if they were no burden to the business but, as indicated above, they will in fact be incurring a substantial and recurring loss.

The appearance of a loss in the accounts when surplus facilities are disposed of is an illusion created by accounting necessities. The loss so recorded probably occurred in reality some months or years before it was recognized in the accounts. The accounting entry simply acknowledges a fact which remains a fact even if the management chooses to retain the surplus resources. The argument may be illustrated in figures as follows.

A machine with an anticipated life of, say, five years, cost £5,000 and was accordingly depreciated in the accounts at the rate of £1,000 a year. At the end of the third year the machine became redundant owing to changes in methods of manufacture, and no further productive use could be envisaged for it in the business concerned. The accounts and balance sheet of the business at the end of the third year showed the following position:

	Machine at cost	£5,000
Less:	Depreciation set off against income for three years at £1,000 pa	3,000
	Unrecovered value in the books	£2,000

It was then ascertained that if the machine were sold it would fetch only £500 and its disposal would in consequence result in a loss of £1,500 appearing in the accounts of the fourth year, thus:

	Book value of machine, as above	£2,000
Less:	Proceeds of sale	500
	Loss	£1,500

Because management were reluctant to see this loss of £1,500 appear in the fourth year's accounts, they decided to retain the machine until the end of its anticipated life when it would be fully depreciated and a profit could be shown on sale. At the end of the fifth year the machine was sold for £100 which appeared in the accounts as a profit:

	Cost of machine	£5,000
Less:	Five years' depreciation at £1,000 pa	5,000
	Book value at end of fifth year	—
	Sale proceeds	100
	Profit	£100

In fact, during its life the machine was costing in maintenance, space, clerical work, etc., an average of £400 per annum, and since it was doing no work during the last two years this cost was pure loss in those years. Assuming that all costs were recovered out of income during the three years when the machine was in productive use, a more realistic profit and loss account for the machine would appear as follows:

	Cost of machine		£5,000
Add:	Maintenance for five years at £400 pa		2,000
	Total costs		£7,000
Less:	Cost presumed recovered out of income during the first three years:		
	Depreciation: 3×£1,000 =	£3,000	
	Maintenance: 3× £400 =	1,200	
	Sale proceeds	100	
			4,300
	Loss (unrecovered costs)		£2,700

But if the machine had been disposed of at the end of the third year, when it became redundant, the profit and loss account would have shown the following result:

	Cost of machine		£5,000
Add:	Maintenance for three years at £400 pa		1,200
	Total costs		£6,200
Less:	Cost recovered:		
	Depreciation: 3×£1,000	£3,000	
	Maintenance: 3× £400	1,200	
		£4,200	
	Proceeds on sale	500	
			4,700
	Loss (unrecovered) costs		£1,500

The foregoing arithmetic could be given greater precision by including interest on capital as a cost and discounting costs after the end of the third year, but the figures given sufficiently illustrate the inadvisability of retaining assets after they have become redundant.

What was wrong with the original accounting was that the depreciation rate originally calculated was too low. On the assumption that neither management nor the accountant could have predicted that the machine would have ended its useful life to the business in three years, the error in calculation was unavoidable, but it was nevertheless a fact. If the future could have been foreseen the annual rate of depreciation would have been calculated in the following manner:

	Cost of machine	£5,000
Less:	Sale proceeds at end of three years	500
	Net cost	£4,500

Annual depreciation $\frac{£4{,}500}{3} = £1{,}500$

At the end of three years the machine could then have been sold without any loss appearing in the accounts and presumably the three years' depreciation and maintenance, etc., could have been recovered in income. The loss of £1,500 at the end of three years shown in the preceding set of figures really represented the deficiency of depreciation in those years (£500 a year shortfall) and this deficiency occurred before the end of the third year when the question of selling the machine arose.

Similar arguments can be applied to the heavy write-down of stocks which periodically occurs in company accounts. These losses almost inevitably refer to previous years when the redundant stock was overvalued. The description 'slow moving' is often applied to stocks which are in fact effectively a liability rather than an asset. When employees are discharged on the grounds of redundancy the payments due under the Redundancy Act (plus whatever additional sums are paid in pursuance of company policy) rarely refer to the period in which the payment is made. They became an effective liability as soon as the personnel concerned were no longer needed for productive purposes. Whilst the retention of redundant personnel has no more economic justification than the retention of redundant plant or stocks, we appreciate that human beings cannot be treated in the same way as inanimate resources. The curious feature of many companies is that they are more ready to discharge redundant people than redundant stocks or useless machines.

A practical illustration

Returning to the example for which specimen figures were given in the last chapter, the measure of the underutilization in the first three years (by the exact, and not rounded-up, calculations of capacity) is as follows:

Years	Output in units	Hours at 3 per unit	Capacity in man hours	Spare capacity in man hours
1	18.2	54.6	176.4	121.8
2	33.2	99.6	176.4	76.8
3	55.1	165.3	176.4	11.1

It will be observed that in this example the calculations are made in man hours on the grounds that in this particular business man hours best represent the capacity of the plant. In different concerns it may be more appropriate to use other factors, such as passenger miles for a transport undertaking, or process hours where the predominant work covers the treatment of materials, and so forth. Even in the situation under discussion it may be that the business is unable to sell its capacity in terms of man hours, in which case the problem must be broken down further. This can be done by calculating the capacity of separate operations, cost centres or works departments, such as the capacity for lathe work, for metal spraying, pressing, etc. In any event, any project for 'filling the factory' will have to be considered in relation to the available capacity of the key operation demanded by the project.

The alternatives now facing the management, if they are to make remunerative use of the spare facilities in the first three years, are:

1 To consider whether sales and output of the main product can be expanded in the first three years.
2 To consider whether another product can be produced and sold.
3 To obtain work of a subcontract nature, either from other companies or from government departments.

In considering these alternatives the management should apply to them in turn the four questions discussed earlier in this chapter. Essentially, the ideal solution is to obtain a *full profit* from the additional work, after accounting for an appropriate share of the cost of existing facilities; but if this is not possible, work which produces a *contribution* would be better than nothing.

Assume that the management is unable to obtain any work which produces the full profit. It may be possible to obtain a contribution by offering sufficient of the main product at a low price to special customers or in particular markets and thus expand output. Because of the dangerous repercussions such a policy might have on the goodwill of the customers who were charged the normal price and on pricing policy as a whole, we will suppose that this alternative is discarded. It is also found impossible to develop and sell a new product in the time available. As is frequently the case in such circumstances, the only remaining alternative is to seek work of a subcontract nature.

Government contracts are generally available only to those companies which have the necessary technical expertise and can otherwise satisfy the authorities that they have the managerial, financial, and organizational competence to perform the work satisfactorily. Thus, the field for government contract work is, very properly, limited and we will assume that the company in question cannot obtain work in this quarter. Considerable subcontracting is carried out by large companies, especially work of a short-run nature and that which would otherwise divert the efforts of management and operatives from the main objective. A new company would have a reasonable chance of obtaining such work if it were able to quote on a contribution basis only.

Suppose that, for the purpose of illustration, the company is able to obtain assembly work from a major company at a price of £4 an hour. According to the figures given in the previous chapter, direct labour costs are £2 an hour; production variable overheads are 50p an hour; administration variable expenses are 30p per labour hour. Since there will be no selling cost involved and material is issued free by the customer, the additional expense to be incurred by the work are likely therefore to be £2.80 an hour, thus providing a contribution of £1.20 an hour. The following table shows the volume of this work which the company is able to obtain and the resulting contribution.

Year	Spare capacity in man hours	Subcontract work in man hours	Value	Additional costs	Contribution
			£	£	£
1	121.8	60.0	240.0	168.0	72.0
2	76.8	70.0	280.0	196.0	84.0
3	11.1	10.0	40.0	28.0	12.0

The company is now in a position to prepare forecasted profit and loss accounts for each of the five years covered by the forward plan. In preparing these forecasts it has been assumed that there will be some natural build-up of the fixed costs until they reach the total expected in the fourth year, as set out in the preceding chapter.

Years	1	2	3	4	5
Main product					
Sales					
Units	17.4	32.8	54.1	56.0	63.1
Man hours @ 3 per unit	52.2	98.4	162.3	168.0	189.3
Value @ £20 a unit	£348.0	656.0	1,082.0	1,120.0	1,262.0
Variable costs – production					
Labour @ £2 an hour	104.4	196.8	324.6	336.0	378.6
Material @ 60p a unit	10.4	19.7	32.5	34.0	37.9
Overheads @ 50p an hour	26.1	49.2	81.2	84.0	94.6
Total production variable costs	£140.9	265.7	438.3	454.0	511.1

continued overleaf

Years	1	2	3	4	5
Main product					
Variable expenses					
Selling @ 80p a unit	13.9	26.2	43.3	44.8	50.5
Admin. @ 30p an hour	15.7	29.5	48.7	50.4	56.8
Total variable expenses	£ 29.6	55.7	92.0	95.2	107.3
Total variable costs and expenses	£170.5	321.4	530.3	549.2	618.4
Contribution from main product	177.5	334.6	551.7	570.8	643.6
Add: Contribution from contract work	72.0	84.0	12.0		
Total contribution	£249.5	418.6	563.7	570.8	643.6
Less: Fixed costs	250.0*	300.0	300.0	300.0	300.0
Operating profit	£(0.5)	118.6	263.7	270.8	343.6

*Note: in the first year the reasonable assumption is made that there will be a build up of facilities towards those required for maximum activity, and for this reason the fixed costs in that year are shown as lower than the amount which has been assessed for full capacity working.

It is clear that the different situations envisaged in the above example are far from exhaustive. Nevertheless the foregoing example provides some illustration of the problems which arise from underutilization of capacity and the possible remedies. In the long run, if it becomes clear that there is no reasonable prospect of using the facilities to the full, the logical remedy is one which few businessmen seem willing to take: to contract the facilities and the business to an optimum size. The example may also serve to illustrate some of the major steps involved in the financial planning exercise.

A further desirable step is to check whether the required *percentage* return on capital is likely to be achieved by the plan having regard to normal retentions of profit which will increase the capital employed year by year. Assuming a 50% tax charge, no exceptional or non-trading expenses such as interest, and 60% of available profits retained, this further step is illustrated by the following table:

Years	1	2	3	4	5
Operating profit as above	£(0.5)	118.6	263.7	270.8	343.6
Less: Taxation at 50%	0.5	59.3	131.8	135.4	171.8
Net profit	£ —	59.3	131.9	135.4	171.8
Less: Dividends at 60% approx.		24.3	52.9	54.4	68.8
Profit retained	£ —	35.0	79.0	81.0	103.0
Capital employed increased by profit retained	£2,000	2,000	2,035	2,114	2,195
Average capital employed over the year	2,000	2,000	2,018	2,074	2,154
%age operating profit to average capital employed	—	5.9	13.1	13.1	16.0

The above figures indicate that in the fifth year, when the business is operating at capacity, the profitability will be slightly above the 15% required by the profit target – a happily contrived conclusion to the illustration but not always so inevitable in practice!

The forecasts will certainly need revision each year so that they are adjusted to the changes in circumstances which will undoubtedly occur; maybe also to changes in management. At each year's revision a further year forward should be projected on the 'rolling budget' principle. It will also be necessary to take into account the level of inflation at the time of revision. The forward plans will be more generally comprehensible if they are initially drawn up in terms of the then current purchasing power of the currency, and adjusted annually in relation to changes which have in fact occurred in that purchasing power. For special purposes, however, such as arranging for forward finance, the future rate of inflation will need to be predicted.

5 Price determination

Current methods

Methods of deciding on the price at which a product or service is to be sold vary widely between different businesses. In many cases it may be said that the word 'method' is a mere euphemism; a complete absence of any scientific method is all too often apparent. In view of the wide range of modern industry and the infinite variety of business situations, the apparently casual nature of many pricing decisions is not particularly remarkable. Yet a small error in the price at which a product is marketed may make all the difference between profit and loss; or at least that error may be the major cause of inadequate profitability. Incorrect pricing policy may cause the failure of the most efficient enterprise.

Pricing decisions are, therefore, an integral part of forward planning and their importance cannot be overemphasized. If such decisions are to be made on a rational basis, it is necessary first to establish the principles involved and then to apply those principles to a given situation. The objective is to ascertain 'the right price' – if there is such a thing – in the particular business situation and for a given period of time. For this purpose the responsibilities and general procedure for determining prices should be clearly laid down.

In attempting to formulate principles and evolve a workable procedure it is helpful to examine the methods currently or traditionally used by a range of business, because the principles on which business operates are more likely to be derived from the facts than by a process of abstract reasoning. The danger is that whilst a traditional procedure may have had a rational basis when it was first evolved, rapid changes in industrial conditions may soon outdate traditional methods. The following paragraphs survey some of the prevailing methods of price determination on very general lines.

Consider first the price charged 'at the end of the line' – by the retailer. Under the old conditions of widespread resale price maintenance, or at least 'recommended prices', the retailer was not overburdened with pricing problems, many of his prices being decided for him by the supplier. His main preoccupation was to ensure that his shelves were adequately stocked with fast-moving goods which provided him with an adequate margin over their cost. This may still represent an effective if oversimplified concept of retailing, particularly so far as the small businessman is concerned, but modern developments have introduced certain new factors of critical importance: the growth of large stores and supermarkets, with branches in the major centres of trade; retail stores operated by manufacturers of the products, as in the clothing trade; the great buying power of these concerns; the effect of rapid inflation. These factors have created intense competition, which is often reflected in price; the small retailer must react to such price competition if he is to maintain the rate of turnover critical to his success. Thus the growth of the large retailer has enforced considerable flexibility in pricing policy and pricing tactics.

Cost price remains the basis for retail pricing and the irreducible minimum below which, save in exceptional circumstances, prices cannot be set. Price flexibility lies in the range of the amount or percentage of profit on cost. It is questionable whether the true cost for this purpose is confined to the supplier's price, for that price does not take into account the heavy expenses in stocking, selling, publicity and administration involved in modern retailing. It is becoming widely accepted that, in a period of inflation, cost should be calculated on the outgoings required for replacing the goods and services, and not on a basis of outdated costs and prices. The difficulty lies in calculating the cost relevant to a *single product*.

On the face of it, the wholesaler's problem is similar to that of the retailer, in that he is not involved in development and manufacturing costs. Frequently the wholesaler has greater discretion than the retailer in the price at which he sells the goods, particularly in the establishment of a scale of trade discounts for his various customer groups and in respect of order sizes. The majority of wholesalers regard price as a function of cost, and for this purpose the cost which is considered is the price paid to the manufacturer for the goods. The important costs of warehousing and transportation are rarely applied in a scientific manner to the exercise of determining a price, except to the extent that they may or may not be covered by the addition of some notional percentage to the buying price of the goods. A further cost of considerable significance for the wholesaler is interest on the capital employed by purchasing and holding the goods, but there is little evidence that this element of cost is taken into account. In any event, as this chapter will discuss, it is open to question whether cost, however ascertained, is the sole or even the most important factor in the pricing process.

The greatest variety of pricing methods is to be found in the vast field of industry outside the retailing and wholesaling concerns. In some concerns the emphasis in deciding a price is on a particular concept of cost and in others on the market or the willingness and capacity of the customer to pay. Where cost is the dominant factor the responsibility for calculating a price, at least as a basis for discussion by other managers, normally rests upon the financial officers; where the market is held to be the dominant factor, the sales or marketing department usually have the major voice. Where government contracts are concerned, the initial quotation is usually prepared by an estimating department, which may or may not be ancillary to the financial function, and the negotiations are often conducted by a contracts department.

The calculation of a price as a result of adding a profit percentage to cost is prevalent in general engineering, especially in the production of components and cushion-built equipment; it is also the general rule in nationalized industries, with some qualifications where prices are decided by international agreement (such as in the air transport industry) or by the dictate of a government board. The cost-plus basis used by the nationalized industries, e.g. gas, electricity and coal mining, is probably the consequence of the power of monopoly or semi-monopoly, allied in some cases to the policy of financing future capital expenditure from current revenue. The comparative simplicity of the cost-plus approach cannot be denied, but it does seem to be dictated by expediency rather than sound principle.

The professed theory supporting the pricing procedure for government contracts is that the contractor shall be allowed a reasonable return on his capital. This implies, firstly, that the capital of a business can be assessed on a universally comparable basis in an era of changing money values (this is in fact not the case and would be extremely difficult to bring about), secondly, that the capital once assessed can be allocated with precision to a particular class of work (an equally difficult operation) and lastly, that the manufacturer is entitled to recover his reasonable costs. The philosophy may be sound, but the practice produces some curious effects. It inevitably means that in the long run the profit will be highest where the costs are highest, and it may therefore be doubted whether the cost-plus approach to price determination tends to produce the greatest industrial efficiency.

In highly competitive industries, such as those dealing in consumer products, the tendency is for the price to be be dictated by the market. Generally speaking, 'the market' means the price currently being charged by competitors for the same or similar goods. In a wider sense it means the willingness of the potential customer to pay; and his willingness to pay depends, amongst other factors, on whether he thinks he can get greater satisfaction by spending the money in other directions, or simply by saving it. Thus, the price obtainable in the market must, in reality, be a concept which has many variations. It is likely to be different for different income groups and for people with different desires, tastes, or susceptibility to salesmanship; it will vary according to nationalities and geographical regions. It will change with changing economic conditions, changing conventions and changing tastes or fashion. The market price is, therefore, not one figure but a complex and ever-changing variety of figures. If the pricing methods of a business are dominated by the market, then these reflect merely an attempt to satisfy the major clientele of the business within an acceptable price range. There may be justification for relying on market forces but it is impossible to say that such a basis gives anything like precision to a pricing decision.

Objectives, principles and factors of pricing

It is difficult to find any universally applicable theory of price determination from the foregoing brief survey of existing practices. Indeed, a review of these practices only seems to indicate their apparent defects. The question remains as to whether this important aspect of forward planning is to be accepted as a process without rules or philosophy. Is the right price dependent on the circumstances of each particular business and the flair of each individual manager who finds himself saddled with the responsibility? Flair is not to be denigrated, but it should always be tested by reason.

In attempting to formulate a philosophy of pricing which may be used as a practical guide to business, the first matter to be considered is the objectives of the exercise. Price is one factor involved in implementing business policy. If the policy is to achieve a large share of the market, to extend the area of operations or the class of customer, then price will be a necessary element in achieving that policy. As discussed earlier, policy must be subordinated to the need for the business to achieve in the long term a certain minimum profit if it is to survive and price is a vital factor in the process of profit making. Thus, it may be concluded that the objectives of pricing are to achieve profit, subject to the dictates of policy. It follows that the pricing process is not merely a mechanical one of adding a percentage to cost, nor does it depend solely on an analysis of the prices ruling in the market; it must be carried out in the awareness of policy and of the profit requirements of the business as a whole.

In other words, the 'right price' is the price which will give a business maximum profits in the long run. If this kind of thinking is out of harmony with a certain body of opinion which regards profits as anti-social, it should be understood that the maximum profit has no rational connection with the maximum price – except, perhaps, in a monopoly. The state has ample power to curb monopolies and to remove a substantial proportion of excess profit by taxation. There is some evidence for saying that it is the low-price product which has produced and is likely to produce the high profit. In short, the incentive effect of the profit motive is likely to lead to economies of cost, greater productivity and lower prices.

Once the objectives of the exercise have been established, the factors involved in pricing must be clarified before any firm conclusions as to principles and methods can be derived. The essential factors are the following:

1 The market.
2 The cost.
3 The volume of sales.
4 Pricing tactics.

The nature of the market in this context has been briefly examined above. What does need some discussion is the nature of *the costs*. The cost which is used by many businesses as either the dominant factor or as an aid in price determination is normally the cost of the product, contract or some unit of the service provided. Unfortunately, the product cost is not an absolute amount of money, even if it could be ascertained with precision. The value stated by the accountant as the product cost will vary according to the conventions and methods he uses for its ascertainment; even if it were possible to unify conventions and methods, this cost would still be a variable figure, dependent on management intentions, the circumstances and organization of the business and, particularly, the volume of output predicted. It is the outcome of a complex system of apportioning the business expenses, many of which are only vaguely related to the manufacture and distribution of a particular product.

If they are calculated on a consistent basis, product costs, at least the manufacturing cost element, represent useful conventions for the valuation of stock and work in progress, and are accordingly essential for the ascertainment of profit. When some portion of the marketing and administrative expenses is added to the manufacturing cost of the product, usually by applying some percentage, the resulting figure gives an extremely rough indication of the cost which should be recovered in the price in the long run. More accurately, all that the product costs disclose is that if the costs calculated for all the products plus some additional amount can be recovered in the price, then a business will show a profit. In spite of its quite artificial nature, the product cost has become such a familiar statistic of business that it has attained a kind of mystic significance, as though it were truth itself. The plain fact is that the business might do better by selling some products below their conventionally assessed cost, and some very much above it. The marginal cost, useful for short-term purposes (if it can be quantified), is quite different from the average cost, and the standard cost is different from both. The unit product cost has very little place in the scientific process of deciding the right price.

The costs or expenses of an integral business unit must be considered in their entirety. Price influences volume, and volume influences each of the various business expenses in different ways and to a different extent. What needs to be considered is the extent to which the business expenses are likely to *change* when different price levels produce different volumes of turnover. Thus, the price, considered as it must generally be from a long-term viewpoint, is a decision which is determined by drawing up variable budgets of income and costs at various price levels within the range acceptable to the market; the *right price* is the one which will maximize profits in the long run. That a price is a long-term decision should not imply that it is unchangeable; but if the decision was right in the first place, then any changes would be those dictated by pricing tactics or changed circumstances.

In particular situations and especially for short-lived products there will be short-term pricing decisions to be made, and these are discussed below because they really represent decisions due to pricing tactics. There is only one strategy for pricing and that is to maximize profit in the long run.

Pricing tactics

There is always a range of prices which are acceptable in a particular market or by a particular customer group. Where the demand is *elastic*, that is, where demand reacts sharply to price changes, a high price is likely to reduce sales and a low price to increase sales. The most profitable price may be high or low and it can be found only as previously suggested, by producing forecasts of turnover, income, and costs at various price levels. Because substitutes can be found for most products, and because individuals have many alternative ways of disposing of their incomes, there can be few products for which demand has no element of elasticity. For some products – those for example which represent status symbols – a low price may well *reduce* sales. Different prices apply in different markets; these markets may be in different parts of the country or abroad, but in some cases they may be close to each other – the street trader normally sells cheaper than the shop a few yards down the road. Thus, there is great room for manoeuvre in price fixing – denoted here by the term tactics.

Tactics are short-term dispositions and they are invoked especially for the purpose of fighting competition. Thus, more use of tactical pricing is found in the consumer products industry than, say, in the steel industry, although the difference is only a matter of degree, not of principle.

Competition imposes on a business the need to maintain its share of the market and the desire to increase that share. Competition can be met by increasing the selling and publicity effort, improving quality and service, or by using price as a weapon. Occasionally, a financially strong company will seek to eliminate its weaker competitors by reducing price below a profitable level and then reverting to the previous or, maybe, a higher price level when the competitors have dropped out of the market. Whatever the moral aspects, this is an extremely dangerous device, and is by no means assured of success because sometimes the smaller and supposedly weaker company may operate more economically and be prepared to accept the lower price. Minor reductions in price for the purpose of increasing the market share and thus obtaining the benefits of larger-scale production are more common and often take a concealed form such as by the offer of gifts and trading stamps. There can hardly be any financial objection to such an operation provided it achieves the objective.

Differential prices to different customer classes are also common features of pricing tactics. The objective may be to increase turnover or to reduce operating costs. Costs will be reduced by production of long runs unhindered by frequent re-tooling and organizational changes in the works to deal with spasmodic orders. For this reason there is often an advantage in encouraging orders from bulk buyers by offering them favourable trade discounts – which is just another way of reducing price. This is the practice in the motorcar industry, and is less of a short-term measure than a customary procedure.

For short-term purposes the price which recovers something above marginal cost will produce a contribution towards meeting existing recurrent expenses and profit. The subject of marginal costing was considered in some detail in the preceding chapter; it does form part of pricing tactics. Pricing to recover marginal costs and profit may be used to obtain a foothold in a market and to maintain facilities during a recession. The short-term finishes when the existing facilities, which give rise to the current expenses, could have been eliminated or applied to some other profit-earning purpose, but it is by no means easy to determine when this point has arisen in relation to a particular item of expense. For this purpose tactical pricing to cover merely additional expenses and a contribution to profit is fraught with great dangers and demands the most careful consideration. One of the more obvious dangers is that the additional customers who obtain the benefit of marginal prices may resell at a price below that charged by the supplier in its basic market. It is imperative that management is convinced that the sales arising from a price based on marginal cost are *additional* sales.

Pricing tactics are of special importance where a new product or service is to be placed on the market. Costs are likely to be high when the product is first launched because (a) initial expenses of technical development and market research have to be recovered and (b) production skills are enhanced as activity rises. Basically, the problem is whether to begin with a high price in order to reap the utmost benefit until competition is encountered, or to begin with a low price in the hope of discouraging competition. A high initial price is more in conformity with the high initial costs associated with a new product, and it does leave scope for price cutting when competition appears. The low starting price will probably mean that profits otherwise obtainable may have to be forgone, and it may not be successful in discouraging competition. Furthermore, customer goodwill may be forfeited when the price is subsequently raised to an economic level. Perhaps the most logical pricing policy for a new product is to begin with the price which is likely to produce the required profit in the long term, and to endeavour to hold that price for the long term. If all companies followed that principle there would, presumably, be no need for pricing tactics.

The approach to price determination suggested in the preceding sections of this chapter can be illustrated by the following example: the launching of the motorcar accessory for which the basic forward planning routines were examined in earlier chapters. In the illustration presented so far an ex-factory price of £20 a unit has been assumed. This section examines the processes by which that price might have been established.

The essential facts of the situation are that a new product is to be launched in a market where there will be some elasticity of demand. The development of the business until a reasonable level of activity is attained is expected to take some four to five years and it is expected to be a year or so before serious competition is met in this particular product line. The object of the exercise is to maximize profit in the long term, which for convenience of illustration is taken to be five years, although plans may well have to be made, at least in embryo, for a much longer term. No overriding matters of company policy are assumed to complicate the simple issue of maximizing profit.

As suggested, the first factor to be considered is the market, and this means (a) the total potential market as it may change over the years; (b) the share of the market obtainable; (c) the range of prices acceptable to the market and their probable effects on turnover. Since it was predicted that the majority of sales will be made to the car manufacturers, the price range ought to be obtainable from them by discreet inquiry. It will be determined by the car manufacturers' appraisal of the extent to which they can pass on the cost of the accessory – which includes the cost of the buying operation and fitment – to their dealers; and it is more than possible that consideration will be given to the effect on the demand for motorcars of installing the accessory. Data on the market potential has been given (chapter 4) and the problem remains of deciding on the acceptable price range.

Market research indicates a rising population of cars in the UK and it is thus necessary to decide a datum point in time at which to assess the effect of price on sales turnover. In accordance with the need in industry for long-term planning, the exercise is conducted on the basis of the potential sales in five years' time. Since the key problem is the price to be charged to manufacturers, estimated production of cars can be taken at this point, amounting to 1,700,000 cars in the year. Research indicates that the acceptable price range lies between £18 and £22 ex factory, and variable budgets at three points within this range are constructed as follows (see facing page).

The £22 price can be eliminated because the profit is low both in amount and as a percentage of the capital required to sustain the level of turnover. The amount of profit is highest at a price of £18, which naturally gives the greatest volume of sales, but the percentage return on capital is below that obtainable with a price of £20 a unit. The amount of profit in relation to turnover depends to a large extent on the 'spread' of the fixed costs (but refer to the previous discussions on the inaccurate nature of the customary division between the fixed and variable headings of cost). This is only the first stage in the budgeting exercise. The decisive factor is the relation between the profit and the capital employed to achieve that profit. The implication of the figures is that a great deal of additional resources are required to sustain activity at 80,000 units a year, perhaps because of a disproportionate rise in stocks and debtor balances involved. The best percentage return is obtained with a price of £20 a unit and this is the price fixed by the company. It will be noted that any assessment of product costs is quite irrelevant to this conclusion.

What has been arrived at is a 'basic price' resulting from a pattern of estimates and data which is of necessity imprecise. This basic price may have to be amended for two reasons; firstly, if experience indicates in due course inaccuracies in the data and secondly, because marketing tactics impose an amendment. Experience may, for example, demonstrate that a wrong appreciation was made as to the strength and timing of competition, and

Price	£18	£20	£22
Sales:			
Units in thousands	80	60	40
Value	£1,440	£1,200	£880
Costs:			
Variable	£640	£480	£320
Fixed	350	300	280
Total costs	£990	780	600
Profit	£450	420	280
Capital required	£2,450	£2,000	£1,600
Percentage on capital	18.4	21.0	17.5

marketing tactics with regard to price may have to be employed to fight the competition.

Dealing with competition may induce the company to charge a greater or lesser price than the basic £20 a unit for a period in the programme. If it is considered that no competition is to be expected for two years, then a price of £22 or even more could be charged, thus enhancing profitability in those years. This is because it is assumed that neither production nor selling resources can cope with more than 40,000 units of the product per annum in those early years. When competition was encountered output would be at a higher level and a sharp reduction in price could be made. On the other hand, it may be felt that competition could be discouraged from setting up manufacturing facilities for the product by initiating sales at well below the £20 basic price but, as mentioned above, this would be a dangerous policy for at some point the price would have to be raised to an economic level. In the original planning a reasonable profit target for this company was reckoned at 15% on capital employed so that there is, in any event, room for some flexibility in price before the return falls to this level.

These tactics are essentially for short-term purposes. If a price of £20 a unit is the one likely to bring the best return on capital to the company, it is a reasonable assumption that it will represent the most remunerative price for another company. This assumption remains valid only whilst the company in question is operating efficiently, but it would be absurd to base prices on excessive costs in a competitive market. Whatever may be the desirable tactics in the short term, it follows that a company basing its pricing methods on the approach outlined above need not fear price competition in the long run, for a competitor could undercut only at the expense of its profits.

Recovering initial expenses in price

A feature of financial planning and control which is of growing importance is the need to recover initial expenses in launching a product or cultivating a new market. *Initial expenses* refers to research and development costs, market research, tooling, the expense of installing new systems, organization and procedures, preliminary publicity, and so forth. In the administrative area the installation of a computer, which is presumably carried out to deal more efficiently with future activities, may also be considered part of the initial expenses of a programme of development.

What most concerns pricing is that these often formidable expenses are incurred perhaps some years in advance of the income or savings which they are intended to produce. Subject to the dictates of prudence, the logical accounting practice is to carry forward these expenses in the accounts and to set them off against future income on some reasonable basis. What is a reasonable basis depends on the value still remaining in the initial expenses, and this means their capacity for continuing to earn income. Thus, in theory at least, research and development costs should be completely written off in the accounts at the point when technological advances have overtaken the original development.

The UK accountancy bodies have recommended that, with some exceptions, research and development expenditure should be written off as it is incurred. This view presumably follows the dictates of prudent accounting and applies to situations where there is no reasonable certainty of the company recovering the expenditure from eventual sales. The recommendation applies, in particular, to the treatment of the expenditure in the published accounts; it should be borne in mind that the extent to which the expenditure should influence price is under consideration here.

When the cost of a product or contract is presented by the accounting services it will usually include a substantial figure which represents an apportionment of research and development, tooling and possibly, though exceptionally, deferred advertising. At the same time, and for reasons of prudent accounting, the current cost of products will include portions of expenditure, such as selling expenses designed to produce future income, which have no real relevance to current sales. Nevertheless, when price is based on cost, such as with contract work, it is customary for the price fixer to ensure that the initial expenses are recovered in the price. The immediate question is whether and to what extent the price in a competitive market should be influenced by the initial expenses or cost of development.

If the system of variable budgeting, advocated in this chapter, is adopted, then the first exercise (that of assessing the acceptable price range in the market) is quite independent of costs. The only point where costs influence the decision is in calculating the likely return on capital at the different levels of turnover which are dictated by selected price levels. The question then resolves itself into the problem of whether the costs for the latter purpose should cover only current expenditure or should include apportionments of expenses which have been incurred and paid many months or years before the income is receivable.

The costs to be included for the purpose will include so-called fixed costs to the extent that they will be payable in future for the purpose of earning the income. In other words, the only fixed costs to be included are those which will be required to keep existing facilities in being to sustain the production and sales. The initial expenses under discussion, including research and development, are of a different nature from recurring costs because they have already been incurred and paid for some time ago. The question is what pattern of activity will produce the greatest profit after deducting *future* relevant expenditure from *future* income, and for this objective past expenditure is irrelevant.

Following this argument, depreciation based on the historical cost of the fixed asset would be excluded from the total of fixed costs. It will be recalled that the present purpose is merely to ascertain the most remunerative price within a price range, and it may well be that depreciation is relevant for other purposes. Depreciation based on historical cost represents an allocation to periods of time, e.g. calendar years, of money spent on plant in the past. It would thus be correct to exclude historical depreciation from the calculation if the life of the product was less than the life of the machine on which it was made, for in that case no future expenditure would be incurred in providing plant to assist in producing the income. But if, as is the usual situation, a machine needed to be replaced during the life of the product, then the cost of replacing it would be relevant, being a future cost. The total cost of the machine is hardly likely to be applicable, however, because normally a machine would be used in the production of a number of products. Furthermore these calculations are made for convenience in yearly periods so that the appropriate proportion of the annual depreciation, based on replacement cost, would appear to be relevant. The amount of such depreciation must be a matter of judgement, and consequently not precise, but its inclusion, if significant, would bring the calculations nearer to the truth.

Much the same reasoning could be applied to research and development and tooling expenditure which needed to be renewed during the life of the product. Past expenditure is irrelevant here, but not future expenditure on necessary further development and re-tooling. Once again there will be considerable difficulties in giving precision to the figures, but these figures are to be used only as a guide to the optimum long-term price, and it is accepted that this guide may need to be qualified by market factors and tactics.

If it is objected that initial expenditure must be recovered in the price of the goods, the answer is that such expenditure must be recovered in the margin between future income and future costs or, in brief, out of profits. Even if the initial expenditure exceeded these profits, it would be better to recover part of the expenditure which had been expended than none at all.

Whilst the above concerns only methods of arriving at a sound pricing policy, it is interesting to note that current methods of inflation accounting for the purpose of the formal accounting statements tend to use replacement costs for depreciation and, indeed, for the cost of sales, as opposed to historical costs. The theme of this book is that the most effective use of accounting for management purposes lies in *the forward projection of intentions and probabilities.*

The 'loss leader'

The *loss leader* represents a marketing tactic sometimes used to stimulate demand for a major selling line. The idea is that by selling a related product at an exceptionally low price the customers will be induced to buy the profitable mainline products. The loss leader may cost more or less than the main product. Thus one way of stimulating the sale of gramophone records is to market record reproducers (this is not to imply that record reproducers are sold at a loss) and one way of increasing sales of beer is to offer tobacco and salted almonds (again, no implication is intended). In some cases the loss leader can become quite a profitable line, but generally it means diverting effort from the main product and is therefore usually costly. Few companies are prepared to admit that they suffer losses on any line of sales, unless they are agitating against government intervention such as the high rate of tax or inequitable hire-purchase restrictions. Nevertheless, the loss leader is a fairly common marketing gimmick and needs careful examination as to its justification from a financial point of view.

The only financial justification for the loss leader is that it increases the return on capital achievable by the enterprise as a whole. Taking the long-term view it is questionable whether a company increases the return on capital by permitting a loss to be incurred indefinitely on the sale of a product. The real question is whether many of the so-called loss leaders are in fact incurring a loss for the company. Because of the imprecise nature of the product cost, as previously explained, the fact that a profit or loss is being incurred on a single product cannot normally be determined by comparing the price with a cost which is the result of a complex system of apportionments. The only effective method of determining whether a loss leader is a worthwhile proposition is to forecast what would happen to the company's overall profit if it were discontinued or sold at a higher price. If the management are proposing to launch an ancillary product on the market at a price below the accountant's estimated full cost, the proposal can be appraised only by considering what will be the overall effect on the company's profit in relation to capital. The problem is not one of costing but of budgeting or forecasting. Profitability cannot really be assessed in relation to a single product where two or more products are included in a selling 'package'; the income, costs and capital involved in the whole selling line must be considered as a whole.

Assuming the foregoing argument is accepted it still remains necessary for prices to be determined in respect of each item in the package. The problem of pricing in these circumstances – which are very common – becomes far more complex than that of pricing a single product, especially if it is agreed that the product cost is always a very rough and often quite misleading basis. The solution is to break down the problem into its component parts. The first stage is to determine the most profitable price and volume at which the business is likely to sell the key product which it was set up to market. This establishes the basic volume; price determines volume not the other way round. Provided the business continues to operate within its economic level of activity, any increase in volume of the key product is likely to increase profits in relation to capital employed. Any increase in volume of sales will almost inevitably increase the capital employed in making them, if only because of the additional funds needed to finance the greater volume of debtors and stocks. If it is thought that the volume of the key product can be increased by marketing an ancillary product, even if the latter is sold at a conventional loss, then the next exercise is to calculate the loss (or conceivably additional profit) likely to be incurred by the ancillary product at various price levels and turnover of that product. The third stage is to consider what effect the various volumes of the ancillary product will have on the key product and, lastly, to find the combination which will increase the return on capital for the whole concern.

To illustrate the above argument, assume that a business making razor blades is contemplating the marketing of a safety razor in order to increase the sales of the main product. The following figures are purely hypothetical and apologies are due to the manufacturers of either or both of these products if the figures are quite unreal.

Assume, first, that the pricing of the main product – razor blades – is derived from the following very simplified variable budgets:

Estimated Sales at three Specimen Price Levels – Razor Blades

(figures in thousands unless otherwise indicated)

Specimen prices per packet	60p	55p	50p
Estimated sales – packets	10	12	14
– value	£6,000	6,600	7,000
total costs	£5,700	6,312	6,694
profit	£300	288	306
Capital employed	£1,500	1,600	1,800
Percentage return	20%	18%	17%

On this basis the most profitable price is 60p a packet with a turnover of £6 million a year. Although the amount of profit is greater with the price of 50p, the percentage return on capital at that price is less than that obtainable at a price of 60p.

The next calculation is to estimate the volume of the loss leader – razors – that can be sold at various price levels and to assess the effect on profits of those sales.

Estimated Annual Sales at Specimen Price Levels – Razors

(figures in thousands unless otherwise indicated)

Specimen prices	10p	7.5p	5p
Estimated sales – units	500	600	800
Value	£50	£45	£40
Additional costs	60	70	80
Margin	£(10)	£(25)	£(40)

It will be noted that the costs shown in the foregoing are merely the additional (or *marginal*) costs likely to be incurred by the business in making these ancillary sales. On the basis that this is a short-term tactic to increase sales of blades, no element of existing expenses is included in the foregoing costs. At this stage the question does not arise of the extent to which sales of razors by themselves add to or detract from profits, but only of their effect on the overall position of the package of sales. The mere fact that the sales at 7.5p and 5p show greater losses than those at 10p is not relevant in itself. It is now necessary to estimate the effect that the various levels of razor sales will have on the turnover of the main product. Assume that these estimates are as follows:

With sales of razors at	500	600	800
Additional packets of blades sold will be	1,000	1,100	1,200

The additional return achievable with these combinations of sales can now be calculated in the following manner:

Sales			
Razors – Price	10p	7.5p	5p
– Units	500	600	800
– Value	£50	45	40
Blades – Price	60p	60p	60p
– Packets (additional)	1,000	1,100	1,200
– Value	£600	660	720
Total additional sales	£650	705	760
Costs (additional)			
Razors	£60	70	80
Blades (assume additional cost at £0.5 a packet)	500	550	600
Total additional costs	£560	620	680
Profit	£90	85	80
Capital (additional)	160	180	190
Percentage return	56%	47%	42%

The answer to the problem is, therefore, to sell razors at 10p each and, by so doing, profits of the company as a whole will be increased by £90 and on the additional capital a return of some 56% is likely to be achieved. Such a solution, on the figures given, might be affected by marketing policy which sought to obtain a greater share of the market irrespective of immediate profits, and in this case it is possible that the razors would be sold at 5p each. The financial planners would, in any event, be unhappy to see the ancillary product unprofitable in itself and in the long run would suggest that efforts be made, by reducing costs or increasing price, to ensure that it 'stands on its own feet' as a viable product. There would be considerable justification for this view if, once it had served its purpose by raising the turnover of the main product, that level of turnover could be held by the selling effort alone.

We feel it necessary to admit, at this point, that the presentation of specimen figures to illustrate an argument, such as those given above, glosses over all the immense difficulties and effort in making the forecasts. Clearly, any attempt to place the pricing decision on a logical basis is bound to contain many errors, due to misjudgement or lack of relevant information. The justification for the attempt is that a logical basis for forward planning must contain fewer errors than mere guesswork. Once a plan has been established and the assumptions on which the plan was formulated have been set on paper, it is much easier to make adjustments in the light of experience. In particular, it is probable that precise effect of sales of the loss leader or sale of the main product will not be known until some experience has been gained after the plan is in operation. Sometimes surprising results one way or the other appear when the loss leader is discontinued. The need for planning does not lessen the need for experimentation in business.

The price of service

The preceding sections set out some guidelines for determining the most remunerative price for the sale of a product, whether it is manufactured by the seller or purchased for resale. However, many businesses sell service of various kinds rather than tangible goods; in such cases the subject of the price or fee is less specific.

Some professional bodies have established systems of fees for identifiable and recurring assignments and these scale fees are presumably based on a combination of the normal time to be occupied by the assignment and the quality of the expertise required. Where such fees are established by a closed profession, the practitioner is not theoretically concerned with the market and not greatly concerned with the willingness or ability of his client to pay. But even in the closed professions there is some evidence that fees are adjusted in relation to the financial position of the client – the market has an influence on price.

For other kinds of businesses providing services, such as in the servicing of equipment or in transport operations, it is common for the charge to be made either in relation to the time taken by the job or for the use of assets and equipment. The servicing of vehicles will usually be charged on the basis of the man hours involved plus the cost of materials used; for transport the charge may be on the basis of the time taken for the use of the vehicles, as in car hiring, or on a combined factor such as ton miles for the transport of goods. In such cases the costing system has a direct application to pricing and uses the same units of measurement.

Although in such cases the price is essentially based on cost, the market must have a strong influence on the final charge to the customer – especially in the form of competitors' prices. Subject to the quality of the service, the customers would soon become aware of where they could obtain the least expensive service and tend to transfer their custom to that enterprise. On the face of it, the businessman providing a service can adjust prices within the range of the normal profit mark-up. He can, if necessary, adjust his price down to a margin above variable costs, provided he can be assured by carefully controlled budgets that his resultant contribution will produce a sufficient surplus to cover fixed costs and profit; but this is difficult to achieve and overshadowed by uncertainty.

The essential problem for the provider of a service is the same as that for the provider of tangible products, and that is to develop a system which will produce a normal price sufficient to give a reasonable return on capital employed. Such a price would give a firm basis for pricing tactics designed to maximize profits.

The attempt to solve this problem relates to the theme of the previous chapter in which it was suggested that all businesses have a capacity to carry out work, and this is measured by the units of the limiting factor capable of being generated. The existence of a limiting factor implies a limitation on the resources available. Profitability is maximized by using limited resouces in the most remunerative manner. It is also a matter of common experience that working at full capacity will produce the lowest costs per unit produced; for present purposes production is measured in terms of the limiting factor. In many service businesses the limiting factor is the number of skilled man hours that can be generated having regard to other facilities of the business; and subject to some complexities. Time is usually the constraint.

The preliminary conclusion for service industries is that price should represent a payment for the use of so many units of the limiting factor. This conclusion will hardly be news to most businessmen in such industries for they traditionally bill customers on the basis of man hours or machine hours occupied on the job. The more difficult question is the amount to be applied per man hour or other unit. Such an amount, it is suggested, should be the total economic costs of the enterprise when working at capacity, divided by the potential units of the limiting factor which could be generated. The level of utilization of capacity at which the business happens to be working is irrelevant for the purpose because the business must be prepared to compete on price with the competitor which is working at capacity and in consequence has the lowest unit cost.

Admittedly the calculation of the total expenditure likely to be incurred by a business working at full capacity may appear a daunting task where the business has never operated at that level. But much of the fixed expenses, such as the cost of occupying the premises and depreciation, will be the same whatever the level of activity. It should be possible to calculate the amount of the variable costs at capacity on the basis of ratios of the key factor, e.g. man hours and machine hours at that level. One additional expense which needs to be included is a minimum return on capital employed in the business on the assumption that in the long run that minimum must be earned or the enterprise will be deprived of capital and eventually go out of business.

The calculation is summarized as follows:

	(thousands)
Capital employed	£1,000
Interest on capital @ 15%	£150
Fixed establishment expenses	850
Contribution required	£1,000
Variable expenses, operating at capacity of 200,000 man hours a year	1,000
Total cost at capacity, including basic interest	£2,000
Pricing base per hour: $\frac{£2{,}000}{200}$ =	£10

The basic price for a job would take the following form:

Man hours	5
Price per hour	£10
Price for the work: 5 × £10	£50
Materials, at actual cost if bought out; replacement cost if from stock	12
Expenses, at cost	8
Basic price	£70

Notes: 1 So that the price base shall be competitive, the hours (or other units representing the limiting factor) should be the standard hours. However, for many services this is a counsel of perfection – the time involved may be virtually impossible to assess. In such a situation there is no practicable alternative but to use actual hours and to endeavour to negotiate the final price after completion of the work; otherwise it will be expedient to incorporate in the estimate a substantial contingency allowance.

2 Depending on the market situation, the basic price would normally be adjusted upwards by the addition of a mark-up for 'true profit', i.e. profit above basic interest on capital which for

present purposes at least is regarded as a cost. In special situations, such as the need to maintain activity and employment in a slack period, it may be necessary to revise the basic price downwards. So that the job shall make at least a contribution towards fixed costs and minimum interest, such revision could be made to the level of variable costs. In the preceding example, this would give a minimum price as follows:

Price for the work:

	Variable costs: £1,000	
5 hours × Capacity	200	£25
Material		12
Expenses		8
		£45

The approach to the formulation of pricing policy outlined above is essentially intended to apply to a business selling an intangible service. There is considerable justification for the contention that businesses selling goods and equipment are also in effect selling services. In the case of merchandising concerns the service consists in the organization which investigates the demand, obtains the goods required and makes them available to the customers. A producing undertaking provides the same services to the customers but, in addition, provides a further service of adding value to raw material and parts perhaps in the form of extracting material, certainly fabricating, processing and assembling. The objective of such enterprises may be said to be to obtain adequate reimbursement for the services it supplies, as distinct from the finished product. On this argument the basic price for a business dealing in goods and equipment is also a price for the services supplied, plus the cost of the material, parts and expenses involved. The price acceptable to the market may well have reference to the product, but the price required by the business is, from this viewpoint, a price for the services supplied. The commercial acumen of the manager lies in reconciling these two viewpoints.

6 Capital budgeting

The scope and nature of the subject

Probably more words have been written on the subject of capital budgeting in recent years than on any other subject relating to financial planning and control in business. It is not the purpose of this chapter to repeat what can be studied in more detail elsewhere. (A short list of recommended books is given at the end of the book.) But it is necessary to prevent the essence of the subject in a book of this kind and especially to emphasize that capital budgeting is an integral part of the process of financial planning in business; it is neither something new nor a specialized technique that can be separated from the ordinary management procedures. The question is not merely that of the application of the mathematics of discounting the cash flow, despite the fact that, unfortunately, 'DCF' has become something of a magic incantation, as though it were the panacea for all business ills.

So far, forward planning has been considered from the viewpoint of the enterprise as a whole, to underline the objective of obtaining a certain return on the capital invested in the business as a single operating unit. In fact, the capital originally invested in an enterprise and subsequently increased by retained profit, is itself re-invested in a vast number of separate, but closely related, income-earning activities and assets. Thus, some of the capital will be invested in plant and machinery and the acquisition of the business premises; some will be invested outside the business, either as a form of diversification, to further the trading interests of the company, or merely as investments of cash, surplus to immediate requirements; and the remainder will be invested in the complex mass of items known as working capital. In addition, there may be investments in the less tangible but equally significant assets of goodwill, patents and trade marks.

The balance sheet by no means shows the totality of investments made by an industrial or commercial concern. An increasing amount of money is spent by companies on activities which are essentially investments designed to produce a future return but which, for reasons of accounting prudence, are written off against current income and not valued. Investments of this nature include the growing expenditure on training and management development, the establishment of improved administrative systems, e.g. computers, public relations activities and publicity in general. The broad definition of 'capital' is expenditure designed to produce future income; strictly there can be few outgoings made by business enterprise in the private sector – except taxation – which do not conform to this definition. In a sense, therefore, all budgeting in business is capital budgeting. The justification for any expense is its likelihood of producing a future reward.

If future returns constitute the justification for expenditure, then the test to be applied to a proposal for spending money is the extent to which such expenditure will yield a profit. A detailed calculation could not be applied to every one of the innumerable business outgoings made on a day-to-day basis, and in any event many of such payments are matters of necessity rather than pre-planning. Business concentrates on the more detailed appraisal of those large investments in fixed assets, from which income is expected to be produced for many future years. It is those items to which the word capital is conventionally applied and it is those which are the usual subject for capital budgeting and discounted cash flow techniques.

In broad terms, the test to be applied to a proposal to acquire a machine, for example, is whether the business as a whole will be better off after the acquisition than it would have been without the machine. 'Better off' can be interpreted in two ways: firstly, will more cash flow into the company as a result of the acquisition, and secondly, will the acquisition add value to the company over and above its cost? Fortunately, in the long term – assuming that all the values are turned into cash – these two concepts will be identical; not so in the short term. An investment in, say, a distillation plant could produce a negative return in the form of net cash inflow for a few years until the liquor has matured and can be sold, but meanwhile the increasing value of the liquor may well exceed the decreasing value of the plant due to physical depreciation. Conversely, an investment in a passenger-carrying coach might produce a good net inflow of cash for, say, three years, but during this period the operators may be losing capital because the net income is less than the depreciation on the coach. Using the last example to take the long-term view-point – in this case over the life of the coach – the justification for its acquisition will be measured by the surplus of:

(a) cash receipts, including the eventual disposal price of the coach; over
(b) the original cash paid for the coach, plus the operating expenses.

In other words, in the long term net cash inflow equates with profit.

An industrial company is a far more complex entity than those used to illustrate the argument above. It does not normally liquidate all its resources at the end of a period, and count up what surplus cash remains. A developing business normally means one that is making continual investments in stock, debtors and further fixed assets, so that its net cash inflow may be negative for long periods although its net worth is increasing. Whilst the cash-flow basis for assessing individual capital projects does give considerable precision to the exercise, the decisive test of any capital project is its effect on the profit-earning capacity of the business as a whole.

In the theoretical discussions of the subject of capital budgeting, great stress is laid on the supposition that for every project of capital investment there is an alternative use of the money. The fundamental truth of this statement cannot be denied for if, say, a machine is to be bought, the money for the purpose must either be withdrawn from an existing investment of its funds made by the company, or it must be obtained from outside as additional capital employed. This assumes the ideal situation where every pound of the company's capital is invested in some income-earning direction; if the purchase is made out of idle funds, say, in the current account in the bank, such funds were not part of the capital *employed* in the business and represent additional funds.

In any event additional funds could have been used to buy another asset, or have been invested in another direction; existing funds could have been left where they were to earn income.

When this theory of the ever present alternative is applied to some business transaction, on capital account, it is not so easy to postulate an alternative. Where, for instance, a steel-making company invests in an electric furnace, there is really no alternative if all its competitors have electric furnaces and it is to stay in business. If an air transport undertaking fails to invest in engine changes for its aircraft at stated intervals, it might as well go into liquidation, for the aircraft will not be allowed to go into the air unless they are airworthy. Businessmen are familiar with many other examples of this nature where it is not so much a question of carrying out detailed arithmetical examinations of projects of capital investment, as of having to make the capital investment pay after the money has been spent.

Where there are alternatives each project needs the most careful appraisal before the money is spent because, if it is found subsequently to have been ill-founded, most of the money will have been irretrievably lost. Even the most scientific and sophisticated system of financial control cannot recover money which has been, so to speak, poured down the drain. Another important facet of this subject is that an increasing proportion of current business expenditure is of the nature of capital expenditure in the sense that it is made with the intention of producing income not this year or next year but, perhaps, many years hence. Within certain limits the wages bill can be tailored to current activity but little can be done in a period of recession about the unrecovered development expenditure made five years ago. In other words forward planning, with all its inevitable imperfections, has become of greater importance to business than systems of control.

Techniques of investment appraisal

Subject to these general observations it is desirable that business managers shall be able to appraise, from a critical viewpoint, the various techniques which may be applied to capital projects. The complexities of the mathematics can be left to the experts; since the answer will be an estimate and an attempt to look into the future, accuracy of figurework is less important than soundness of principle. All techniques relate the return to the original investment. The major difference of approach is that some businesses relate expected profit (in the sense of additional value) to the investment, and others relate the cash flow to the original investment.

The rate of return (profit)

The traditional device of relating expected profit from a capital project to the original investment is frequently dignified or vilified (according to the axe being ground) as the 'rate of return'. All this means is that someone has to budget for the profit which is likely to emanate from the project, after charging depreciation and making such accruals and deferments of expenditure as accord with normal accounting principles. The forecast will be made for a number of years and each year's profit shown as a percentage return on the capital; or, conceivably, the profit will be averaged over a period of years and the return computed from the average. This method, which is probably still used by most businesses, has been subject to severe criticism by the theorists, largely on the following grounds:

1 The charging of depreciation is 'double-counting' for it represents the original cost of wasting assets spread forward over their expected life. Thus, the capital cost of purchasing the plant, etc., is counted once in the capital investment and again in the computation of profit. The accusation of double-counting is somewhat weakened with modern methods of inflation accounting whereby depreciation is calculated on replacement cost as compared with historical cost. The implications of inflation accounting for depreciation are that funds are being set aside for the replacement of the asset and the charge is no longer to be regarded as an allocation to future years' accounts of an historical cost.

2 In any event, depreciation is very much of an approximation, the annual amount depending on an estimate of the asset's useful life and on the convention (e.g. fixed instalment, diminishing balance etc.) used for its calculation. Furthermore, the de-

preciation charge is often, though quite wrongly, influenced by matters of managerial policy and taxation.

3 The rate-of-return method takes no account of the fact that profits expected to accrue in some years' time are not worth so much as more immediate profits. Thus, it is impossible to compare two or more alternative projects. Assume the profit estimated to accrue from two alternative methods of investing £100,000 is as follows:

Forecast profits *Years*	*Project A*	*Project B*
1	£5,000	£15,000
2	15,000	20,000
3	25,000	20,000
4	30,000	20,000
5	35,000	30,000
Totals	£110,000	£105,000
Average per annum	22,000	21,000
Average %	22%	21%

On the face of it, project A is superior, but project B has the merit of producing substantially greater profits in the first two years when, incidentally, the forecasts should be more exact than in the later periods. In fact, it is impossible to distinguish between the two investments on the figures alone.

Cash flow

The alternative to using the profit as a return on the investment is to forecast the cash flow and relate this to the investment. It is important to consider the nature of cash flow, and its distinction from 'profit' in the usual sense, if the techniques outlined below are to be soundly appreciated. The term *cash flow* is frequently used by financial journalists when examining companies' published accounts and the figure they are using is profit plus depreciation. This is quite a notional concept because it cannot under any normal circumstances equate with the net addition to the cash resources of the company which occurred during the year under examination. It is true that the charging of depreciation in the accounts on the basis of historical cost has no effect at all on the cash inflow or outflow because depreciation simply represents an appropriation to the current year of cash spent on the purchase of equipment some years before. Even if depreciation is regarded as a provision for replacing the asset, the charge does not affect current cash flow but is, in a sense, an anticipation of a future cash outflow. The charge against income will have an effect on the amount available for payment of a dividend. Nevertheless, during the year the business may have depleted its cash balances by making increased investments in stocks, debtors, plant and other assets, and increased its cash by obtaining credit from the bank, trade creditors and elsewhere. It would be possible to agree that profit plus depreciation represents the net amount which will eventually flow into the company's bank account, were it not for the fact that the accounts will include a large number of other deferred charges as well as a number of prepaid expenses, none of which affect the cash flow in the period in which they appear. At best, therefore, profit plus depreciation is a very rough approximation of cash flow.

The more common-sense view of the meaning of cash flow is the difference between cash receipts and cash payments in the period. This is precisely the figure the accountant seeks to determine when he prepares his cash forecast, a very normal and essential exercise in financial planning. The cash flow in the latter sense will rarely if ever equate with profit for the reasons given in the preceding section. It is well known that profitable businesses have failed merely because of inability to pay their debts, or deficiency of cash flow. A developing business will normally experience a negative cash flow because it is continually making further investments in stock, debtors, fixed assets, and other resources. A contracting business may well have a positive cash flow and be embarrassed by excessive liquid resources which it is unable to use, because it is in process of liquidating its assets in stocks and debtors and outside investments.

The main justification for the cash flow approach to the appraisal of capital projects is that cash is the commodity which can be used for making further investments. It is a mistake to imagine that profit can be invested; profit is simply a measurement of increased value, cash is something tangible. The secondary justification for using the cash flow approach is that the cash flow from two or more alternative investments can be reduced in each case to a single figure for comparison purposes, by means of the discounting process.

The receipts used for the cash flow calculations will not therefore be the same as the sales and other income used for calculating profit, for the following reasons:

1 Some of the receipts from customers will refer to previous years' sales, and some of the current year's sales will not be paid until after the end of the year in question.
2 Receipts will cover items other than normal trading income, e.g. receipts from sales of redundant materials and plant and investment grants receivable on the purchase of equipment.

Likewise, payments will not correspond to the charges shown in the profit and loss and other revenue accounts because:

(a) the revenue accounts will contain charges which were paid in prior periods;
(b) some of the charges shown in the revenue accounts will not be paid until after the end of the year concerned. This will be accentuated by the modern tendency for charges such as the cost of sales to be calculated on a replacement basis.

In particular, the revenue accounts record the cost of materials (and other added values) consumed, whereas the cash account covers payments actually made in the period, whether the materials or services were used in that period or not.

Taxation aspects

Frequently when making investment appraisal calculations the effect of taxation is brought into account on the grounds that the profit or loss from the project will affect the taxation payable by the company, and thus the net cash flow derivable from the project. For this purpose it will be necessary to calculate the addition to *taxable profit* (not the same as accounts profit) resulting from the project, and to provide in the cash flow calculations for the payment of the additional tax when it becomes due and payable – such point not normally being the same as when the profit was earned. If, as is likely, the project includes the acquisition of plant and machinery, then the taxation liabilities of the company will be affected by the capital allowances on those acquisitions.

Many taxation allowances, especially capital allowances, were expressed to be designed to encourage industry to invest in more economic plant. Unfortunately the complexity which taxation introduces into investment appraisal calculations does not have quite the same incentive effect; a project which originally appeared to be satisfactory could become uneconomic if tax rates and allowances change, as they do every year or so.

Another complexity is that the incidence of taxation can differ according to the financial situation of the company concerned. A company with tax losses one year would not in that year obtain the benefit of capital allowances and make a project of capital investment unjustified, whereas when the tax losses had been absorbed that project could become viable. Projects undertaken by a small company could become uneconomic when the company grew into a larger undertaking and became liable to higher taxation. For similar reasons a specific project could be justified for company A but unjustified for company B, owing to different tax liabilities of the two companies.

For these reasons the propriety of including taxation in calculations of capital projects could be questioned. Are there more fundamental arguments for ignoring taxation in this context? One such is that taxation is levied on the company's taxable profits as a whole and it is generally impracticable to apportion that tax with any degree of precision to each individual project. Another argument is that a company's tax liability may be regarded as the somewhat arbitrary share of that company's profit which accrues to the government – on a par with the dividend paid to shareholders which would certainly not be included in an investment appraisal calculation. The legal minimization of taxation is an exercise as important as capital budgeting, but quite separate. A project which is worth while in the sense that it will earn a satisfactory profit should not be rejected on the grounds that a certain proportion of that profit will be payable to the government.

Thus taxation brings an unfortunate complexity into the comparatively simple operation of calculating the expected cash flow from an investment; this complexity cannot be ignored. The general conclusion must be that, for the purpose of appraising a single project, taxation should be ignored. However, this would not be valid when the question is one of deciding between alternative uses of the money available, where because of taxation effects project A could be shown to yield a greater net present value than project B. This difference could occur, for example, where the alternatives lay between the purchase or the hiring of plant.

Merits and demerits of the cash flow approach

So much for the nature of cash flow which, as emphasized above, needs to be clearly understood by managers if they are to use the approach purposefully and realistically. Its disadvantages are rarely discussed by its advocates, but may be briefly expressed as follows:

1 It takes little account of increasing values which, although unliquidated, are being built up in a business.

2 It takes no account of the fact that year by year assets are depreciating, although in the long term this depreciation will be evident in the cash flow when further sums have to be expended to replace assets.

3 Its assessment involves many complexities, such as forecasts of when payments will be made for assets and services and when cash will be received from sales. However, this is hardly an additional chore because a cash forecast will constitute an important part of any competent financial plan.

The advantages of using the cash flow approach are these:

1 Once the assessment has been made, the concept of the difference between cash received and cash paid is more easily comprehended than that of profit, which involves the application of a number of conventions and matters of judgement and policy.

2 Cash flow is vitally important to business for it is the figure which is available for reinvestment to earn further income.

3 Cash flow is amenable to the discounting process which simplifies comparisons of alternative investments. It may be noted in this connection that it is hardly logical to discount profit because this is simply an assessment of increased value, not necessarily in liquid form. The major justification for discounting is to find the sum which, if invested at compound interest, would accumulate to the cash flow in the given period.

Discounting the cash flow

Assume that projects A and B, of which specimen profit forecasts have already been given, were assessed on a cash flow basis, and that the assessments were as follows:

Forecast cash flow

Year	*Project A*	*Project B*
1	£1,000	£(5,000)
2	16,000	5,000
3	30,000	30,000
4	35,000	45,000
5	45,000	55,000
Totals	£127,000	£130,000

The difference between the above purely hypothetical figures and the estimates of profit might be due to the following reasons:

1 Cash flows are lower than profits in the earlier years because in those years substantial payments are made in building up stocks and equipment and there are inevitable delays in receiving payments from customers.

2 In the later years cash flow exceeds profit because money is now being received for past sales and the build up of facilities is tailing off.

3 The cash flow from B exceeds that from A because B is in a development area where investment grants apply.

4 Higher depreciation for A has reduced profits.

On the above figures the cash flow approach makes B the better investment, contrary to the indication of the profit estimates. The figures have been contrived to give this result, but it is quite a possibility for the reasons given above. A more valid picture will be given if the cash flows are discounted.

The principle on which the discounting of cash flow rests is that income due in the future is not worth its face value at the present time. This is partly because 'what's to come is still unsure', but more specifically because interest can always be earned on a present sum of money and it will grow to a larger sum in the future. If a business sold goods worth, say, £1,000 at the present time and agreed to give a year's credit subject to 10% interest, the amount receivable in a year would be £1,100. In other words, at 10% interest the present value of £1,100 due in a year's time is £1,000; the cash flow of £1,100 due in a year has been discounted back to its present value of £1,000. If two years' credit were given and interest were payable annually, so that it could be reinvested at 10%, the amount receivable in two years would be calculated as follows:

Present value	£1,000
Interest for one year at 10%	100
Due in one year	£1,100
Interest for second year at 10%	110
Due in two years	£1,210

Thus, the present value at 10% of £1,210 due in two years is £1,000.

The acceleration in the growth of an investment on which interest is compounded, as indicated by the above very simple illustration, is well appreciated by businessmen. What is sometimes not so clearly appreciated is that precisely the same process must logically occur in reverse; that is, when a calculation is made of the present value of a future payment or receipt. This is because the present value or the *discounted cash flow* is the sum which, if invested now at the given rate of interest, would amount to the increment of cash in the period concerned. It follows that the present value will decrease as the rate of interest rises. The present value of £1,210 due in two years at a 20% rate of interest is £840. The present value will fall the more remote the increment of cash becomes. The present value of £1,210 due in twenty years' time is only about £101. Assuming that the validity of the cash flow approach to the appraisal of a capital project is accepted, the conclusions to be drawn from the facts stated above are:

1 Managers should consider with particular care the justification for the use of a high rate of interest in these calculations because (a) a high rate may make a perfectly viable proposition appear to be uneconomic and (b) it may exaggerate the difference between two or more alternative projects.

2 It is unnecessary to carry the forecasting of the cash flow too far, say, beyond 15 to 20 years – because the remoter increments of cash will have little value.

3 A really long-term project, of which the main benefits are not expected to accrue until far into the future, must produce a very high return indeed in those future years before the discounted cash flow technique will show it to be worthwhile.

As indicated, discounting the cash flow has the great practical merit of simplifying the comparison between alternative projects, because it enables all the increments of cash to be reduced to one figure of present value for the whole project. This is demonstrated by the following example which uses the figures of cash flow given above.

Discounted cash flow – interest at *10*%

		Project A		Project B	
Years	*10*% factors	Cash flows	Present values	Cash flows	Present values
		£	£	£	£
1	0.909	1,000	909	(5,000)	(4,545)
2	0.826	16,000	13,216	5,000	4,130
3	0.751	30,000	15,020	30,000	22,530
4	0.683	35,000	23,905	45,000	30,735
5	0.621	45,000	27,945	55,000	34,155
		£127,000	£80,995	£130,000	£87,005
Deduct: Original investment		100,000	100,000	100,000	100,000
Surplus/(deficiency)		£27,000	(£19,005)	£30,000	£(12,995)

It is now apparent that, at the given rate of interest, neither project is worth undertaking for each results in a deficiency.

Apart from the inevitable inaccuracies inherent in the forecasts, a major element of uncertainty in an exercise of this kind is the rate of interest. A different rate might give a contrary answer, as using 5% instead of 10% will make clear.

		Project A		Project B	
Year	5% factors	Cash flows	Present values	Cash flows	Present values
		£	£	£	£
1	0.952	1,000	952	(5,000)	(4,760)
2	0.907	16,000	14,512	5,000	4,535
3	0.864	30,000	25,920	30,000	25,920
4	0.823	35,000	28,805	45,000	37,035
5	0.784	45,000	35,280	55,000	43,120
		£127,000	£105,469	£130,000	£105,850
Deduct: Original investment		100,000	100,000	100,000	100,000
Surplus/(deficiency)		£27,000	£5,469	£30,000	£5,850

Thus, the decision as to the appropriate rate to use can be of vital importance and the unfortunate manager who has to make the decision is presented with the following alternatives:

1 The rate actually payable by the company to finance the project. This basis sounds simple enough, but could apply only where the project represented a separate business which obtained its own finance. Where the project was just one of a number of operations conducted by a particular company, it would usually be impossible to ascribe a particular 'parcel' of finance to one project. Even if further money had to be borrowed before a project could be put into effect, the need for the money could equally well be attributed to heavy drawings on cash caused by antecedent operations. In any event, the interest now payable for finance may and almost certainly will alter in the future.

2 The current average rate payable by the company on loan capital. Such a rate appears to be somewhat more realistic, but it does

mean that if many projects were instituted on the basis of the average borrowing rate the company might not be able to meet its full interest charges.

3 The target rate of return aimed at by the company. If this rate could be achieved for every project, management's problems would be largely solved, but the adoption of such an ideal return would tend to exclude from consideration a number of promising projects of investment.

4 The rate which the company could obtain on an alternative investment carrying equal risk. This is probably the theoretically correct answer to the problem, but it does involve the difficulty of assessing the risk. Furthermore, in many situations the company will have no alternative but to embark on a project of capital investment in order to maintain its competitive position.

The problems involved in deciding on the suitable rate of interest can, fortunately, be overcome with a little more effort by using the yield method which is described in the next section.

The yield of a capital project

Instead of beginning with a rate of interest as a basis for the calculations the *yield* method arrives at a rate of interest as a conclusion to the exercise. It then remains for management to decide whether the rate of interest which is produced by the investment is adequate in relation to the yield obtainable from alternatives. This rate of interest is that which, if used for the purpose of discounting the cash flows, will make their total equal to the original investment. The difficulty is that the only method of arriving at this yield rate is by trial and error. Using the figures already given, one would assume that the rate of interest required for the purpose will lie somewhere between 5% and 10%. Assume the present values of the cash flows discounted at 7% was the first attempt and then, because this – as will be seen below – produced too low a figure, the next attempt was made at 6%. The figures are as follows:

Project A

Year	Cash flows £	7% factor	Present values £	6% factor	Present values £
1	1,000	0.935	935	0.943	943
2	16,000	0.873	13,968	0.890	14,240
3	30,000	0.816	24,480	0.840	25,200
4	35,000	0.763	26,705	0.792	27,720
5	45,000	0.713	32,085	0.747	33,615
	£127,000		£98,173		£101,718

It is now clear that the answer lies between 7% and 6%, and in fact it will be found that a rate of 6½% will produce total present values of nearly £100,000 (actually £99,936). Accuracy to within ½% should be quite sufficient for an exercise of this nature which can only be based upon a number of assumptions as to the future. In fact, it might be desirable to present the original forecasts of cash flow in two tables, one showing the minimum and the other the best possible forecasts. This would mean calculating two extremes of yields of which the truth, as so often happens, lies somewhere in the middle. If managers are presented with a maximum and a minimum target, human nature may well be satisfied with achieving the minimum.

Project B

Year	Cash flows £	6½% factor	Present values £	6¼% factor	Present values £
1	(5,000)	0.939	(4,695)	0.941	(4,705)
2	5,000	0.882	4,410	0.886	4,430
3	30,000	0.828	24,840	0.833	24,990
4	45,000	0.777	34,965	0.785	35,325
5	55,000	0.730	40,150	0.739	40,645
	£130,000		£99,670		£100,685

The yield of project B lies between 6¼% and 6½%, as shown above, and all that the figures demonstrate is that it appears to be marginally inferior to project A, thus finally settling the question. Note: the yield method tends to be unpopular with the theorist largely because, with certain exceptional combinations of figures, it is possible to produce two yields for the same list of cash flows. Such an exceptional situation is unlikely to be met in practice.

Conclusions

Various additional mathematical and statistical devices can be applied to the appraisal of a project of capital expenditure for the purpose of allowing for risk, dealing with probabilities, discounting the effect of inflation, simplifying the calculation of the taxation allowance, and so forth. These devices are the subject of specialist books on the subject. When all the figurework has been done the decision rests with one or more business managers. Whether or not to go ahead with this proposal is the simple question that the manager must eventually determine. In making his decision it is important that the manager puts the figurework into the right perspective. The figures and the mathematics are nothing more nor less than aids to the decision-making process. They aim to give the utmost precision to the factors and tendencies which the manager must put into the balance when making his decision. So much has been written in recent years in support of the discounted cash flow technique that there is a danger of managers becoming hypnotized by the figures and the mathematics. It is necessary to bear in mind that the apparent answer shown by the figures depends entirely on the validity of the original estimates.

In a few cases the forecasts will tell so clear a story from the outset that there will be little need for further calculations; the project may be obviously desirable or obviously uneconomic. It is where the success or failure of the proposal is not crystal clear from the beginning that one or more of the techniques described in this chapter can aid the decision. In some cases the figurework may indicate that a project is not worthwhile, but if the development of a product, the acquisition of new machinery, the cultivation of fresh markets are essential for the survival of the business, such a proposal must be made to pay however unfavourable the forecasts and arithmetic may appear. The final decision to go ahead is unlikely to be decided on the figures alone: the human qualities of determination and enthusiasm on which an industrial enterprise really depends for its success are factors which inevitably and rightly will be brought into the balance of judgement.

This is not intended to denigrate the use of figures, indeed management would be foolish to ignore them, but it is necessary that their limitations be clearly understood if they are to be effective tools in management's hands. The major problem in the use of figures for the appraisal of a project of capital expenditure lies in the dilemma between the profit and the cash flow approach. In spite of all the academic writing in favour of discounted cash flow, there are sharp differences of opinion amongst accountants and businessmen as to the merits of the two approaches. Business must make profits and at the same time must achieve a favourable cash flow. In some businesses – heavy industry, for example – plant is long lived and depreciation, however difficult its assessment, represents a very heavy recurring loss of capital. It cannot be ignored as it is in the cash flow techniques. Many businesses are not seeking a high cash flow, but are more interested in the growth of assets. On the other hand, in a business where there are, or ought to be, frequent replacements of plant, the cash flow approach will automatically take account of the cost of further acquisitions and it will be unnecessary to consider depreciation in the reasonably long run. In many concerns the flow of cash is of vital importance. For these reasons, in the consideration of any project of capital expenditure a business would be well advised to prepare forecasts of both anticipated profit and of cash flow; and, because of the problems associated with the rate of interest, the yield method is the best technique for dealing with the latter.

The writing on this subject tends to deal with techniques for the appraisal of individual projects. However, the capital budgets need to be treated as integral elements in the whole forward plan. All the budgets are interdependent and all the expenditure budgets make claims of differing weight on the financial resources of the business. A proposal for the purchase of a new machine should be written into the forward plan so that management shall have the opportunity of deciding whether the financial resources of the business are better spent in making the acquisition rather than, say, engaging more salesmen or installing a function of value analysis. Not every conceivable purchase of equipment can be foreseen, but when an unbudgeted proposal for capital expenditure comes up for approval it means in effect a complete rebudgeting exercise.

7 Organizing for budgetary control

Nature and objectives

So far, the discussion in this book has been concentrated largely on forward planning. The preparation of a plan for the future, although it may well be a salutary exercise in itself, is in essence merely the preliminary to the more positive function of control. *Control* implies *action* – the action of managers in so controlling the affairs of the business that the plan is carried out. As the authors have endeavoured to demonstrate, it is necessary in the interests of efficiency – which means economy of effort – that the exercise of forward planning shall follow a logical routine and conform to a flexible system appropriate to the particular business concerned. It is equally necessary for the practical exercise of control to be formalized into a system which is capable of adaptation to the frequent and sometimes unexpected changes which occur in circumstances external to the business.

It hardly needs stating that control cannot be carried out effectively in a haphazard manner. In any substantial business it is impossible for a manager to carry in his head all the matters which may need his attention, and even if this were possible it would be very difficult for him to deal with them in the correct order of priority. The natural approach is to deal first with the problems which are easiest of solution, unless one is constrained by a system which forces attention to the most important matters. Even if a manager believes that he is aware of the priorities which relate to his own department, he may not be giving proper attention to the priorities of the business as a whole. A production manager may, for example, believe that the reputation of his own department depends upon every effort being directed to maintaining the output of the standard product whereas the overall requirements of the business may demand that he give the greater part of his time to organizing the production of a new product.

What a business needs is a system which (a) coordinates the activities of the various managers in relation to the corporate plan; (b) allocates responsibilities for the action required to achieve the planned results; and (c) indicates priorities. This is the real substance of a system of budgetary control, which has been defined as 'the substitution of considered intention for opportunism in management' – although we doubt if opportunism should be entirely neglected in a dynamic concern. Unfortunately, budgetary control is often associated with the spectre of a cost-reduction programme, often administered by accounting staff who are somewhat remote from the functions of making and selling goods and services. In fact, budgetary control is concerned not only with costs but also with income and, indeed, all the activities of the business. Budgets are basically quantitative measurements of activity related to time periods – so much output in a week, so many sales in a month, the number of goods to be bought, and so forth.

It is necessary that these quantities shall be translated into monetary figures because the end result must be profit and cash.

In brief, budgetary control embraces the following managerial – not purely accounting – activities:

1 The preparation of a forward plan for carrying out the objectives and the policy of the organization, and the expression of that plan in quantitative and monetary measurements.

2 The allocation of responsibilities by means of functional and departmental budgets, for achieving the plan.

3 The formulation of standards for processes and operations, whether they are of a productive, marketing, or administrative nature.

4 The creation of an information service which is capable of prompt and effective comparison between standard and performance for each subdivision of the enterprise. This also involves the analysis of significant variations from the plan so that the manager's attention shall be directed to the areas which need action, thus fulfilling the concept of 'management by exception'.

5 The establishment of a system for revising the plan when such revision is dictated by external changes or amendments to corporate policy and objectives.

organizational structure

One of the most important functions of the manager is to control performance, in other words to intervene as required in the events of the business. If this function is to be carried out effectively and without duplication, it is clearly necessary that each manager's responsibilities shall be clearly defined in the organizational structure of the business. But for the purpose of planning and control it is not sufficient merely to publish an organization chart indicating who is the production manager, the sales manager, the chief accountant and their subordinates. The wider responsibilities referred to include participation in the planning process of the organization as a whole, the vitally important operation of collaboration between departments for the purpose of achieving the corporate plan, and the control of events within each department. Thus, a manager is accountable, not only for the efficient functioning of his own department, but also, jointly with his colleagues, for the achievements of the business as an entity. The second area of accountability will, on occasions, involve deliberate deviations from the agreed programme of output, purchases and sales, when external changes so necessitate.

In the modern complex business a manager may be said to have a tripartite responsibility: (a) to control the costs of his department or cost centre in relation to the volume and quality of the activity which is required of him; (b) to carry out his function of designing, buying, making, selling, or administering in relation to the corporate forward plan; (c) to adjust the scope of his activities in coordination with other departments when external events or changes in policy so dictate. Although we have previously emphasized the need for forward planning to be expressed in the precise terms of monetary targets for each department and for the business as a whole, common sense suggests that it is impossible for the human mind to foresee every detailed happening which will affect future business operations. Budgetary control imposes targets which should be pursued until they become impracticable, at which point planning should be undertaken afresh. Replanning takes time and meanwhile it would be foolish, for example, for the factory to continue producing goods which the collapse of a market has rendered unsaleable.

Subject to the considerations outlined above, what is required of the organizational structure is that each manager's responsibilities shall be made perfectly clear both to that manager and to his colleagues. The budgetary system will then express those responsibilities in monetary terms. This means that every item of expense, every classification of income, every item of capital expenditure, should be charged to the responsibility of specific individuals, and that they should be made accountable for the actual expenditure or income in relation to the budgets. Difficulties will certainly arise in strictly applying the system of accountability and, indeed, of organization which is necessary for budgetary control. Whilst no particular difficulty, other than a mechanical one, will arise in deciding that a manager has fallen short on his budgeted performance, it will not be so easy to determine the extent to which a particular manager's failure to adjust his activity to the prevailing circumstances has caused a budget variance for the whole company. What may be at issue in the latter case is the joint responsibility of the managers *as a team*; for although budgetary control will always be seeking to define responsibilities within precise boundaries, they must inevitably overlap to some extent in a dynamic business.

In their book *The Management of Innovation*, Burns and Stalker have attempted to categorize business concerns as either 'organic' or 'mechanistic'. The latter is the stable, bureaucratic form of organization where responsibilities are clearly defined and rarely alter; the former is typical of a business which is constantly subject to technological and other change and where, in consequence, responsibilities change likewise. 'In the organic system managers are anxious to know what they are supposed to be doing,' say the authors and, of course, this situation is anathema to the exponent of the virtues of budgetary control, where everyone's task needs to be clearly defined. Nevertheless, Burns and Stalker acknowledge that businesses with an organic type of organization will eventually tend towards stability.

In applying budgetary control to an organic business organization, whatever may be the play of power and authority, the present and intended future performance of the different business functions *must* be ascribed to individual managers, otherwise planning and control will tend to degenerate into an uncoordinated free-for-all. It may well be that in the budgetary system a manager is allocated responsibility for certain costs or income when he has only recently assumed authority over the function concerned. In no case has a manager, even in a mechanistic or bureaucratic organization, complete control over the operations he is required to manage. The fact that certain sales are below budget may not be the fault of the sales manager but may be due to inadequate deliveries from the works. The works may be in arrears because of lack of materials. The buyer may be unable to secure delivery of the materials because the suppliers have not been paid. Shortage of cash may be due to a credit squeeze.

Many a system of budgetary control falls into disfavour with the managers because it attempts to turn a budget variance into a personal aspersion on the manager concerned. In some cases, this is the fault of the accounting officers who arrogate to themselves the right to control, without either the authority or the knowledge for so doing; it is only the managers who control, and who must control as a team. The necessity for ascribing costs, expenses, and other statistics of performance to individuals is that they shall account for variances between budget and actual. That is to say they must be prepared to give reasons for the variances and, one hopes, to suggest the remedial action. Ultimately, however, the remedial action will lie with the management working as a team. Thus, a shortage of sales compared with the budget *may* be due to some inadequacy in the sales department, and may be capable of remedy by that department alone. More probably it will be due to a chain of circumstances which demand further efforts in various directions by a number of departments. If the facts are to come to light, someone must be accountable and take the responsibility on his shoulders. The obvious person is the one whose performance has suffered.

The requirements of the accounting service

The first stage in the formulation of an effective system of budgetary control lies in the organizational structure of the business; in particular to define the responsibilities of the managers as individuals and of the management team. The next step is to ensure that there is an efficient information service. Since this service will ultimately be concerned with monetary values it may be considered to form not so much an extension but an integral part of the accounting service. In a small business the administration of the budgeting system may form part of the duties of the accountant, but in a substantial business it is usually necessary to create a separate section.

The accounting function thus logically divides into (a) the recording section which collates and analyses outgoing expenses and incoming revenue and (b) the budgetary section which deals with management's plans for incurring expense and earning income. Because budgetary control is essentially concerned with the accountability of individual managers for performance, the normal organization of an accounting system which records income by categories of sales and expenditure by categories of expense, processes, and operations, will not be appropriate for the purpose. The section of the accounts department which is concerned with historical records must, therefore, produce a further set of accounts by responsibility headings. Many managers are reluctant to concede the necessity for creating this third cross-analysis of 'responsibility accounting', which they tend to regard as another 'unproductive' expense. The result is that the accounting officer is forced to compromise by adapting for budgetary purposes the accounting system created for compliance with legal requirements or for costing uses. The normal form of 'departmental accounts' found in many businesses is quite unsuitable to determine the accountability of a manager because it usually contains an enormous number of apportioned expenses quite outside the control of the manager concerned. The consequence is that immense effort is spent by managers and accounting staff in attempting to reconcile apportioned figures with responsibility, and the whole system falls into disrepute.

With modern systems of electronic data processing, and particularly the advent of the microprocessor, the capability for rapid and voluminous recording and analysis has been immensely widened, and has become worth while for quite small concerns. Small subsystems can be set up within departments and can be embraced by an integrated system for the whole of a company's information requirements. It must be acknowledged that the benefits of a budgetary control system cannot be obtained free; an effective information service can be as valuable an investment as the acquisition of a machine in the factory or a fleet of salesmen's cars.

Even where the recording section of the accounts department is organized to produce figures representing managerial responsibilities for comparison with budgets, the effort will be wasted if the information is not hot on the heels of the events. A recurrent and absolutely justified criticism of the accounting function in business is that the figures are produced too late to be used as a basis for managerial action. There is some (but rapidly diminishing) justification for tardiness in the production of accounts which have to be audited and to conform to a large body of legal rules and accounting conventions, e.g. the year-end accounts for publication. The reason for delay lies frequently in the need to make decisions of policy, to investigate commitments which require provisions, and to decide reserve and dividend policy. None of these complications need affect the provision of information as to the performance of individual managers provided that modern techniques are used and the recording process is maintained on a day-to-day basis. In essence it is a question of deciding in advance precisely what information is required and then organizing a system which will fulfil the requirements.

The information required will depend entirely on the nature and scope of the budgetary system and hence upon the organization of the business by managerial responsibilities. It is a mistake to imagine that a *pro forma* set of budgets applicable to every business can be stated in a book. Much will depend on the type of business and the special aspects of forward planning and control which demand the concentrated attention of the management team during the planning period. Thus, for a certain period a business may be suffering from a fall in demand for its products and management might decide that the remedy, which must be enforced by the budgetary system, is tighter control of operating costs and/or overheads. In another situation, inadequacy of turnover may be due to inability to obtain materials in the quantities required and in this case the buying function and stock control may be given emphasis.

Subject to the foregoing qualifications, a broad picture of the kind of budgets required in a manufacturing business may be given by the following chart:

Chart of Budgets

1 Revenue budgets

A MARKETING DEPARTMENTS' BUDGETS

1 *Orders receivable*, analysed by the main categories of sales and, as necessary, by sales districts, distinguishing home from export sales.

2 *Deliveries* (i.e., sales to be recorded in the accounts) in quantities and value, analysed as above.

3 *Marketing expenses*, covering:
(a) Sales administrative sections;
(b) Field force and district officers;
(c) Market research;
(d) Advertising and publicity, including exhibitions and demonstrations.

B RESEARCH AND DEVELOPMENT BUDGETS

1 *R and D administration*, including, as appropriate to the business, basic design department; drawing office; project engineers; model shop; experimental shop.

2 *Existing projects.*

3 *New projects.*

C PRODUCTION DEPARTMENTS

1 *Overhead* (or indirect) cost of the various production departments, both direct and indirect departments.

2 *Output*, analysed by the same categories as used for the sales analysis, showing quantities, hours (man-hours, machine-hours, operating hours, etc), and cost divided into the main elements, e.g., labour, bought out parts, sub-contract charges, and raw material.

D MATERIAL CONTROL

(In many undertakings these budgets will fall within the production manager's authority; in others, where the function is of particular importance, a material controller, not directly responsible to the production manager, but closely collaborating with him, may be appointed).

1 *Orders to be placed*, analysed by the main categories of materials and production parts, expressed in quantities and values, and scheduled by required delivery dates, distinguishing between direct and indirect purchases.

2 *Deliveries* analysed by the same categories as in D1 above.

3 *Stock levels*, in quantities and value, after accounting for stock-in-hand, deliveries receivable, and deliveries to production departments. Frequently, the stock budgets are compiled by the budget or accounts department on the information provided by the production budgets and the buying programme.

4 *Administrative costs* of the various departments falling under the material control heading, including buying, stock control, stores, and goods inwards.

E ADMINISTRATION

This category of budgets would cover all the various departments embraced by the generic term 'administration', including accounts, communications (telephone, postal services, messengers), typing services, security, personnel.

F MANPOWER

These budgets would be prepared by the personnel department, based on the requirements of all departments, showing the planned recruitment and estimated leavers, analysed by various grades and by departments. Separate budgets would need preparation for education and training costs and a separate programme prepared for management development.

G FINANCIAL COSTS AND INCOME

These budgets would be prepared by the financial department and would show interest payable, discounts receivable and payable, royalties, pension scheme costs and those of other employee benefits, and professional fees. The forecasting of interest payable would depend on the cash forecast, which is considered in the next category. Taxation provisions would also fall within the field of financial budgets, but the estimated taxation charge could not be assessed until (a) the taxable profit for the period had been arrived at, and (b) the capital budgets had been prepared, the latter affecting capital allowances and investment grants obtainable.

2 *The capital budgets*

The methods and approach relating to capital budgeting have been considered in the previous chapter. These budgets would be based on departmental estimates of requirements in the area of capital assets, e.g. plant, instruments, vehicles, furniture, fixtures, and these estimates would, in turn, depend on the nature and scope of each department's future activities. Some of the acquisitions would be for short-term requirements, but many of them would normally relate to long-term plans. The replacement of assets would form an important element of the capital budgets and in this connection estimated residual values of the assets to be replaced would need to be assessed. The capital budgets would obviously be of vital importance for cash forecasting, especially for the planning of long-term finance. The investment grants obtainable would be of importance in this area of budgeting.

The category of 'capital budgets' may be taken to embrace the provision of fresh capital and the redemption of existing capital in the form of redeemable debentures, preference shares, and loans. If the financial position of a business is to remain healthy, it is essential that the investment of resources in both fixed and current assets is subject to careful budgeting and control. Thus, capital budgets would include the economic levels of stockholding. Likewise, investments, both those of a temporary nature and those of a more permanent nature, such as investments in subsidiaries, would represent an important aspect of the financial planning process.

To summarize, a typical capital budget would cover the following headings:

1 Fixed assets.
2 Investments.
3 Stocks.
4 The provision and redemption of capital.

3 *The master budgets*

The term 'master budgets' indicates the presentation of the whole system of revenue and capital budgets in summarized form. In essence, this means the preparation of forward or projected final accounts, including, as necessary, manufacturing and operating accounts, trading and profit and loss accounts, the appropriation account, a cash forecast, and a balance sheet projection.

If these statements are to be effective as guides to the progress of the business in relation to the budgets they must be prepared at frequent intervals and, ideally, comparisons between budget and actual results submitted to the management within a few days after the end of the period which they cover. Many concerns find it desirable to prepare the master budgets, or projected accounts, by monthly intervals for, say, six months, and thereafter quarterly for the remainder of the first year. The longer-term budgets normally cover yearly periods. Long-term budgets should cover five years as a minimum, but a number of businesses find it essential to express their long-term plans by means of reasonably precise figures for many more than five years ahead. The need for long-term planning on a 'total' or corporate basis has been emphasized in earlier chapters.

Organizing the reporting system

It has been suggested earlier that the mere act of preparing a budget is in itself a salutary exercise. This is because the budgetary procedure induces managers to consider, first, the efficiency of their own functions and, second, the effect which their decisions and actions are likely to have on the activities of their colleagues in the business. Moreover, the final integration of the departmental budgets in financial terms makes the managers appreciate that their plans will constitute connected parts of a corporate plan for the business as a whole. The translation of intentions into the exact language of quantities, hours, and money, enforces precision of thought.

The exercise of preparing budgets may well have the virtues mentioned above, but it achieves nothing by way of controlling actual performance. Control is exercised by the action of the managers, not by accountancy. The accounting service can aid the process of control by indicating to the managers involved the extent to which performance is not according to the plans. The first step in this process is to compare performances with the budgets and to highlight the variances. But in providing signposts for corrective action the accounting service must do something more than compare one figure with another. In brief, the duty of the accounting function (which may take the form of a budget section or management accounting section) may be set out under the following headings:

1 Analyse the differences (or *variances*) between budget and actual results.

2 Investigate and report on the causes of the variance.

3 Suggest alternative courses of action to remedy defects in the performance.

In analysing the variances between a standard and an actual figure of income or expense, it is necessary to appreciate that every monetary figure in the accounts of a business is composed of two elements, a quantity and a price or rate. Thus, if the budgeted sales of a product for a period are £1,000, this figure

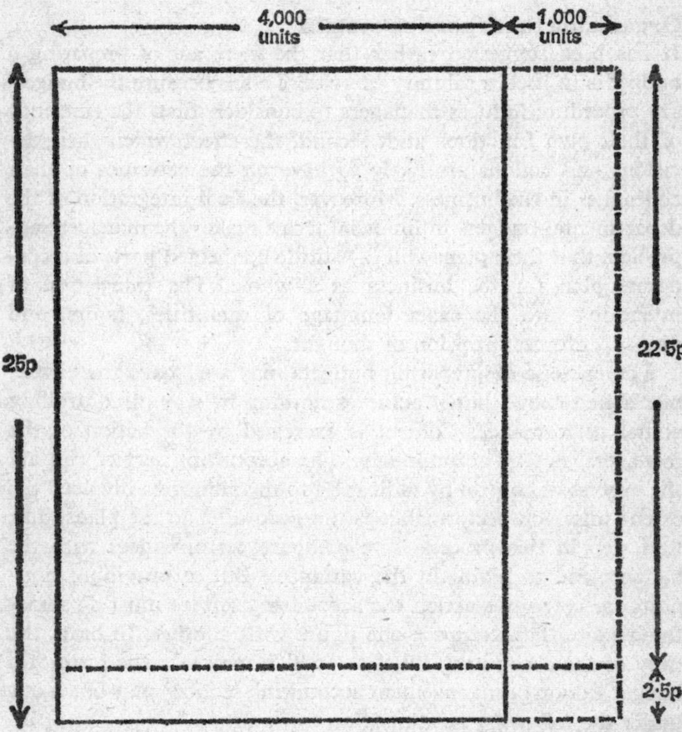

will have been derived from a forecasted quantity of units to be sold, say 4,000, and a forecasted price per unit, in this case 25p. Assume that the actual sales turnover achieved in the period for this product is £1,125. It is not now sufficient to say that achievement is £125 above budget or a favourable variance of 12½%; the £125 may be made up of two figures, one a variance of volume and the other a variance of price. Assume that the actual sales of £1,125 were made up of 5,000 units sold at 22.5p, then the variance of £125 can, in turn, be broken down into the element due to the quantity difference and the element due to the price difference. In fact, there are three variances, as shown by the diagram on the previous page (although for convenience the accountant will normally use only two).

The three variances demonstrated by this diagram are as follows:

Price: 2.5p × 4,000 units	= £(100)
Volume: 1,000 units × 25p	= 250
Joint (price and volume combined):	
1,000 × 2.5p	= (25)
Total =	£125

For simplicity, these variances may be expressed as two items, by using the convention of assuming that the difference in price refers to the actual quantity sold, thus:

Price: 2.5p × 5,000 units	= £(125)
Volume: 1,000 units × 25p	= 250
Total =	£125

The important point to observe is that the mere statement that sales exceeded the budget by £125 conceals two important facts, each of which may have an influence on any decision: first, that value has been lost by reducing the price below that originally budgeted, and, second, that value has been gained as a result of a 25% increase in sales volume. Subject to investigation of the actual circumstances, it is possible that no reduction in price was necessary in order to produce the substantial improvement of actual sales over those budgeted and, in any event, it appears on the face of it that the budgeted standard needs reconsideration – such reconsideration to take the form of a reassessment of the balance between price and volume which is likely to produce the greatest profit.

The above example refers to income in the form of sales, but it is likewise necessary to break down costs and the variance between standard or budgeted costs and actual costs, into their price and volume elements before any valid conclusions can be drawn from the figures.

Assume that the standard cost associated with the sales discussed above was 15p a unit. The budgeted profitability of this line of sales would then have been shown as follows:

Sales:	4,000 units @ 25p	=	£1,000
Cost of Sales:	4,000 units @ 15p	=	600
	Budgeted profit	=	£400

Suppose that the actual cost was 17.5p a unit, then the cost variance (adverse) on the actual sales is 5,000 units @ 2.5p = £125. If the budget and actual results were set side by side with no further analysis, the position would appear as follows:

	Budget	*Actual*
Sales	£1,000	£1,125
Cost of Sales	600	875
	£400	£250

All that is revealed by this statement, as it stands, is that although sales turnover is up on the budget, costs appear to have risen out of proportion to the increase in sales, with the result that profit is down on the budget by £150, or no less than $37\frac{1}{2}$%. Such a conclusion would be inaccurate and misleading for in fact the difference of £150 in the profit compared with the budget is composed of four distinct figures:

Additional income due to increase in sales volume: 1,000 units @ 25p =	£250	
Less: Additional costs due to increase in volume: 1,000 units @ 15p	150	
Additional net income due to increase in volume:		£100
Deduct: Loss of income due to –		
(*a*) reduction in sales price: 2.5p × 5,000 units	125	
(b) increase in costs: 2.5p × 5,000 units	125	
		250
Fall in profit compared with budget		£150

Thus, the first priority in organizing an efficient reporting system is to ensure that facilities are available for the prompt reporting of the results; and the second is to arrange that the variance between budget or standard and actual are analysed at least by the price and volume aspects. Very much more sophisticated methods of variance analysis have been developed by accountants, particularly in relation to standard costing. Information on this somewhat technical subject may be obtained from the large number of excellent publications on standard costing. We are concerned more with the broad essentials than the detailed analyses which can be produced.

Clearly, the arithmetical analysis of budget and actual variances is a comparatively mechanical process which can be reduced to a routine to be performed by staff of limited skill. A further requirement of an efficient management accounting service, and one which requires staff of somewhat exceptional quality, is the investigation of the causes of the variances. The importance of providing such a service is that operating managers, whose main tasks are to direct the functions of engineering, buying, making and selling, should be able to concentrate on these tasks without the distraction of time-consuming investigations or clerical exercises. This is a question of cost. It is less wasteful to employ a skilled man for such investigation at a good salary, than for a half-dozen managers to be spending a large proportion of their time on such matters.

The type of person or persons engaged for the specific purpose of reporting to managers on the major variances which have occurred, and the reasons for those variances, necessitates careful consideration. The technical skill required for the purpose demands not so much an exceptionally high level of technical accounting expertise as a wide and balanced knowledge of the different business operations and processes. With the recent liberalization of the accountant's training in the direction of management and analytical skills, the most likely candidate for the position envisaged is a young accountant with experience in industry. It is by no means out of the question that a man qualified professionally or by a degree in, say, production management or marketing, would not be equally suitable, provided that such a person also has a sound knowledge of business accounting, including costing and budgetary control. A further desirable quality is that the person selected for the task shall have exceptional qualities of tact and the determination to pursue an investigation to the end. Investigations of the nature under consideration are often carried out with enthusiasm by trainees of adequate calibre.

The final requirement of the accounting service is to suggest a course of action to remedy the variances. This is the ultimate service which the accounting function can provide to aid management and is a matter for the more senior financial executives, in consultation with the operating managers concerned. The essential point which this section is endeavouring to make is that the substantial effort and time expended in the budgetary process is in danger of being wasted unless resources are organized in advance for providing management with the necessary information when the actual results are compared with the budgets.

The budget periods

It has become traditional in business to consider budgeting as consisting of two closely related but otherwise distinct exercises: one, to compile the short-term budgets and the other, the long-term budgets. There is no natural dividing line between the two periods and the distinction is made largely as a matter of administrative convenience; the exercise is often so exhausting that it must be taken in two separate operations. We have emphasized earlier in this book the mounting need for more long-term planning in business, essentially because of the increasing amount of investment which is involved and on which a return must be produced over many future years.

On the assumption that long-term planning is essential to indicate at least the general direction which an organization must follow, it is strange to observe that in many cases the long-term plan emerges out of the short-term plan. Assuming that the situation in a business is not one of crisis which demands the immediate attention of all managers, then it is suggested that the *first* budgetary exercise is to produce a long-term plan. It is only when the general direction and policy of the organization has been decided for many years ahead that it is possible to set up standards for the shorter period which must place the organization on the right path.

The long-term plan must be preceded by a statement of long-term objectives, such as the objective of extending a company's sphere of operations on a worldwide basis, or one of complete vertical integration. Allied to the statement of objectives there should be clear announcements as to the policy to be adopted for meeting the objectives. In this context the word 'policy' can have a very wide meaning but, for example, the objective of creating a worldwide organization could be accompanied by a policy of acquiring majority interests in overseas concerns. Once the objectives and policy have been stated, there now remains the practical exercise of formulating a system of integrated budgets which will of necessity be on broad lines. It will follow much the same procedure as is required for the creation of short-term budgets, i.e. it will be the product of a team of managers rather than the brainchild of an imaginative accountant.

The essential question which then arises is: what is the long term? This question is not answered, as it seems many managers suppose, by applying the test of how far the management can see ahead with reasonable precision. If that were the test, long-term planning would probably die in its infancy. The real test is the period which it is estimated will be required for the business to attain the long-term objectives. An objective to raise the size of the business to the level of the largest dozen concerns in the country, which is by no means out of the question as an objective, might well be estimated to take twenty years. A secondary test, which will set the lower limit of the long-term planning period, is the time which will elapse for the existing assets, other than land, to depreciate to NIL value or to become obsolete. It is over that period that the investment in the assets must be recovered with interest.

The foregoing paragraph does little more than indicate the approach to the problem of setting the duration of the long-term budgeting exercise; but at least it does serve to narrow the limits in which the solution must lie. The traditional long-term budget period of five years will, for example, be quite inadequate for an investment in a mine, an oil rig, or a system of undersea cables. On the other hand, and subject to the objectives of the business as a whole, five years may be more than adequate for the long-term planning of, say, a new type of food preparation, a drug, or an electronic device, if each of these examples is likely to be overtaken by changes in taste, fashion, or technology within that period.

To take another and simpler example from the field of the small business, the small shopkeeper rarely looks ahead beyond the coming year, if that. In fact, the durability of his investment, which is, to a large extent, goodwill, depends in many cases on the time which it will take before a chain store is set up in his neighbourhood.

Long-term budgets normally take the form of annual projections of the profit and loss account, the balance sheet, and the cash forecast, with such supplementary schedules as are necessary.

Short-term budgets are frequently expressed in terms of calendar months for a year ahead, or in thirteen periods of four weeks each. In any event, due to the incidence of public holidays, many of these periods are not comparable with each other and the effect of the differences in working days can be extracted by the accounting service in the form of calendar variances. Since output, sales, and direct costs can be calculated to take account of the effect of public holidays, but many overheads will continue unaffected, the calendar variance becomes a measure of the extent to which overheads are 'under-recovered' due to this factor.

Many items comprising the budget will need attention more frequently than monthly periods and this would be the case where the key factor of success is, for example, the rate of weekly sales or the day-to-day efficiency of a factory operation. For such purposes the basic periods on which the budgets are constructed, and the comparisons with actual performance extracted, will need to be weeks or days. If this is the case, then the information service must be organized to provide the comparisons with correspondingly greater speed; the statements should be on the desks of the managers concerned the day after the end of the period concerned. Unless this is done the figures will become history and the effort expended in compiling the budgets and producing the information will be so much unproductive time and expense.

It is customary for the short-term budget to cover a company's financial year, e.g. from 1 January to the following 31 December; or from 1 April to the following 31 March. The convenience of harmonizing the company's budgetary period with that for which the annual accounts are drawn up for the inspection of the shareholders, and other interested parties, is obvious. The cycle of twelve months does, in addition, cover the seasons, which is of evident importance to a business affected by seasonal influences. It is, however, a curious fact that a number of businesses are saddled with a financial year which ends in the middle of a seasonal period, either one of peak sales or of low sales. Except in the few cases where a business is so dependent on the Christmas trade that the season may be said to end effectively at 31 December, a year ending at the latter date rarely embraces a full cycle of selling and manufacturing effort. Certainly, the short-term budget period ought to embrace the 'natural' business year and there is usually little difficulty in making the financial year conform to that period of time.

In some situations it is probable that a period of twelve months is too short and has the effect of making a quite arbitrary termination to the logical short-term planning period. Cases in point are where a business has embarked on the development of an invention, a new product, or the exploitation of a particular market. In such a situation the period of development which will absorb the planning and controlling energies of the management team may well endure for considerably longer than twelve months. The time which it takes for the earth to move round the sun may be quite irrelevant to the venture in hand. The budgeting period may well be eighteen months, or even a number of years, before a product is launched and achieving the desired basic level of sales. This is the period which will require a concentration of real management effort, and at the end of it the venture can be left to the administrator as a matter of routine; it may be called 'the project period'.

Revision procedure

It is a truism that performance never conforms to the budget; or, if this is the case, then it gives rise to the suspicion that the budget has been contrived to make it easy of achievement. Budgeting is not simply an exercise in attempting to predict what will happen, but in giving a direction to an organization and establishing standards of achievement. If these standards are to maintain their validity in a constantly changing world, then arrangements must be made to revise them from time to time. The major question is: how often?

In spite of the importance of forward planning, managers must have ample time to pursue their control function; and, indeed, the hard facts of business life necessitate that a considerable proportion of a manager's time be devoted to routine business. Thus, it is undesirable for revision of budgets to be carried out too frequently even if performance is diverging considerably from the plan. Some businesses revise short-term budgets at quarterly intervals; but it may be observed that so frequent a revision is due to the fact that little revision is normally required, so that the exercise is not unduly onerous. Others revise short-term budgets at half-yearly or annual intervals as a matter of routine; and revise the long-term budgets annually.

It is a natural and commendable human practice to look afresh at the future each year, but it is questionable whether there is any particular logic in carrying out the revision process at more frequent intervals merely as a matter of routine. The essential point is first to define the circumstances which may make revision of budgets desirable or necessary before deciding at what intervals the revision exercise shall be carried out. If we take the purely hypothetical situation that the original budgets were soundly based, that performance conformed to the budgets and that no changes occurred in external circumstances, then there would never be any need for revision. It follows that budgets need revision when one or more of these conditions no longer obtains. The one false element in the argument is, however, the implication that budgets need to be revised when performance is above or below the standards set. This seems to be a prevalent notion in business, but its adoption makes nonsense of the budgetary system as representing standards of achievement, incentives for effort or devices for encouraging the coordination of functions. If budgets are simply altered because they have not been achieved the business would be better without them.

The other two conditions for revising budgets remain, i.e. when errors in their compilation are discovered and when external circumstances make them impracticable of achievement. If these are the only two valid reasons for revising budgets, then they should be revised when either or both of these factors have caused the budgets to be no longer capable of achieving their objectives. The variances between budget and actual due to these causes can and should be extracted and shown separately by the accounting service and it is these *uncontrollable* variances which will in the course of time indicate that revision is called for. Thus, if managers are to use the budgetary system as an effective tool, the revisions should not be undertaken as a matter of routine, at stated periods of the year, but when the situation calls for revision. This attitude would help to make forward planning and control a continuous rather than a spasmodic process.

A budget will need revision, as suggested above, when the assumptions as to external circumstances on which it was based are no longer true. The increasing, and usually unpredictable, government intervention in industrial life will often invalidate the assumptions on which a company's budgets were compiled; this will occur, for example, when changes are made in hire purchase regulations, when markets are arbitrarily diminished by import and export controls, by exchange control, and by restrictions on credit. Large-scale strikes, wars, and rumours of wars – even sometimes the more mysterious changes in taste and fashion – may all have fundamental repercussions on the nature of a company's activities. The rate of inflation is difficult to predict. In the long term these changes should not be allowed to alter the company's overall profit plan or its broad objectives. Minor changes should not even affect the short-term profit plan, except to the extent that circumstances dictate changes in the amount of capital employed in the business. What is required is a change in the pattern of the budgets, maybe also a minor change in policy which is designed to produce the same overall result in terms of the return on capital. This view may be somewhat academic; but the point is that if a business does not at all times pursue its overall objective it will be at the mercy of every economic hurricane that blows from time to time. The managerial function is to overcome circumstances.

Disasters occur which no human ingenuity can wholly overcome. The budgets then become quite worthless and are best omitted from all statements. Until new budgets can be compiled, the financial information can be related only to past figures as a basis for evaluation unless some immediate and temporary forecasts can be substituted quickly. Rebudgeting will take time and mature consideration of the new situation; some months may pass without adequate standards for comparison of performance. In this situation a temporary service can be provided by the accountant with a firm grasp of the realities outside his professional expertise; and this service should take the form of provisional estimates of likely income and expenditure. There are many occasions in business when the formal budgetary system will break down, but the managers will still need some standards, however approximate, against which to measure their performances.

One workable basis for quickly preparing provisional standards of expense is to relate the expenses in the various departments to appropriate units of activity. Thus the allowable expense of a sales department could be related to orders taken;

the cost of a wages department to numbers of employees; the overhead cost of a works department can be reasonably related to the number of units or direct man hours produced. The type of expense in question is that which is controllable and largely 'variable'; the truly fixed expenses of the business will presumably remain unaltered, except by management dictate, until sufficient time is available to construct a new, formal budgetary system as required by the changed circumstances.

8 Essential information for control

What financial information does a manager require?
Managing directors often take great pride in displaying the thick binder of financial information which they receive each month. Their filing cabinets may be bulging with routine and *ad hoc* reports from various subordinates, much of it repeating the same information with a different emphasis. If they are efficient they read very little of this massive documentation, but they find it comforting to know that 'every question man can raise is hidden somewhere in the files'.

If this situation exists it implies three defects in the control system:

1 The managing director will have the greatest difficulty in finding the key factors in the business which merit his attention.

2 Much of the cost and effort involved in producing the information has been wasted.

3 All but the current reports are history and should be destroyed.

Much the same criticism can often be applied to departmental managers who tend to accumulate vast quantities of outdated figures in their search for the elusive evidence of what they should be controlling.

The purpose of this chapter may now be clear. It is to suggest that the financial information which a manager needs to digest is comparatively small; it should be confined to the essentials on which action is needed. These requirements will be satisfied only when:

(a) Managers can rid themselves of the fear that without voluminous data they will be overlooking some inefficiency for which they may be called to account.

(b) They have organized an information service on which they can rely to provide them with the essential and only the essential facts.

So much for the generalities. The difficulty lies not so much in isolating the essential information but in deciding what are the key figures in a particular set of circumstances. In one situation, for example, the key problem may be to correct the sales mix, in another to improve product efficiency, or to maintain liquidity, or to speed up the development of new products. Nevertheless, it is possible to suggest certain fundamental statistics which, with differing emphasis, must be available in most industrial concerns.

Requirements of general management

When planning the financial information service there is some logic in beginning with the requirements of general management since those requirements are likely to decide the nature of the information to be demanded by subordinate managers. If, for example, the current key problem for a business is to expand turnover, then it is likely that sales and production managers will have to explain movements in the figures of sales and output supplied to general management and they must, accordingly, receive information for this purpose.

The 'need to know' on the part of general management (normally represented by a managing director or general manager) falls under two distinct headings: profit and liquidity. If both of these aspects of the business can be shown to be healthy by the aid of some easily understandable statistics there is no advantage in the managing director poring over a mass of supporting figures, and he can concentrate his attention on the furtherance of company long-term objectives. If either profit or liquidity is unsatisfactory, then additional supporting information will be required to indicate the source of the problem and possibly the action required.

The importance of general management concentrating attention on profitability and liquidity is, perhaps, too obvious to need justification. It may, however, be appropriate to mention that the existence of an adequate level of profitability reflects, amongst other factors, the economic utilization of resources. If the profit plan is being achieved there is little point in the managing director examining, as a monthly routine, the detailed figures in the balance sheet showing how the funds of the business have been applied for the purpose of profit; nor need he, in these circumstances, examine detailed analyses of sales or costs. There are bound to be inefficiencies in particular production, marketing and administrative operations, but these are matters for the attention of the functional managers concerned.

Since, in any substantial organization, the managing director is effectively in command of a limited number of reasonably distinct enterprises (represented by the major divisions or product groups) it is necessary that he be provided with information as to the profitability of each group or division, so that he can assess their effects on the corporate performance.

The effectiveness of the information service to concentrate management's attention on the essentials will depend to a large extent on the existence of sound budgets and standards against which performance is to be compared. Ultimately, however, this process of comparison is not completed by recording and commenting on the difference between quantities and sterling amounts. The final expression of the forward plan is in terms of relationships between figures, i.e. percentages.

Example 1

During a given budgetary period the capital to be employed by a company is assessed at:	£1,000,000
The profit target for the same period is:	£100,000
Giving a return of:	10%
The actual profit achieved was:	£108,000
this result was considered more than satisfactory because it shows the profit target having been exceeded by:	£8,000
In fact, due to an unexpectedly greater retention of profit in the preceding period, the capital employed in achieving the profit of £108,000 was:	£1,200,000
So that the percentage return was:	9%
the result was in fact relatively unsatisfactory.	

Example 2

The budget of debtors at the end of a period was:	£400,000
The sales for the period were budgeted at:	£2,400,000
So that budgeted debtors represented:	2 months' sales
The actual debtors were:	£375,000
Which apparently represented a saving in funds of:	£25,000
However, the sales were:	£1,800,000
So that debtors represented:	2½ months' sales
the result was similarly unsatisfactory in that more funds than necessary had been absorbed by the outstanding debtor balances.	

General management and profitability

Group A. Profitability of the capital

THE FIRST STATISTIC: PERCENTAGE RETURN ON CAPITAL EMPLOYED

This percentage is the overall measure of success and should be the first figure to be considered. The following points need to be borne in mind:

1 Because of the inevitable fluctuations which occur in the activity of a business and, indeed, because of the varying speed with which the data is processed, the percentage covering a single month's operations is of little value. The ratio should be calculated over a period of trading which covers normal short-term cycles and usually this will be the last twelve months. However, directors are obliged to account to the shareholders at the end of each financial year, as a minimum, so that, in addition, the percentage should be calculated on a cumulative basis for the financial year of the business.

2 The percentage calculated on the actual results is subject to the severe qualification that it is by no means always calculated on the current monetary value of the capital employed; indeed, if it were so calculated the values used would be bound to contain matters of opinion. A 10% return obtained in a newly established business may be comparable to a 20% return in one in which the fixed assets are valued at the historical cost of many years ago, less

depreciation. Thus, the percentage takes on significance only when it is related to a standard, and that standard should be the percentage return which ought to be obtained in the business calculated as the result of a detailed process of budgeting.

3 Any variation from the budgeted percentage should be capable of explanation mathematically by the subsidiary percentages which are next for consideration. However, exceptional circumstances, such as a recent and unbudgeted increase in capital which is not yet productive, may have qualified the validity of the comparison between the budgeted and actual percentage, and these circumstances should be noted.

4 Since the profit will be on a cumulative basis, and will be continually increasing capital employed until distributed as dividend, the capital employed should be averaged for the purpose of the calculation.

5 The stage of profit which it is suggested should be used in calculating this ratio is *operating profit*, i.e. the surplus before charging:

(a) finance charges, such as interest payable;
(b) exceptional items which are outside the normal trading operations, such as damages in a lawsuit;
(c) items which refer to other periods of account, such as 'book' profits and losses on the sale of fixed assets, and adjustments of provisions;
(d) direct taxation, e.g. income tax and corporation tax.

6 The percentage return on capital employed should also be developed for each division or major product group, so far as it is reasonably practicable to allocate the capital of the whole corporation to these categories. If these percentages are used as measures of comparative profitability between divisions and product groups, then arrangements must be made to ensure that the capital allocated to each is valued on a comparable basis; and this will normally mean a valuation in terms of current money values.

Note: there is a great deal of argument as to whether 'capital employed' for the purpose of calculating this primary measure of success should consist of total assets or assets less liabilities other than loan capital. In *Managerial Accounting* by J. H. Rossell and W. H. Frasure (Charles E. Merrill Books Inc, Ohio) it is said that: 'From an economic point of view the use of total assets as the "capital" of a business is more broadly meaningful for measuring the performance of management. It is the *total* assets of a company ... which are available to management in the operation of a business.' Nevertheless, whatever may be the economist's standpoint, the management of an industrial enterprise is responsible for providing a reasonable rate of return on the shareholders' capital, plus the contractual rate on loan capital; and shareholders' capital plus loan capital = net assets (not total assets). It is also true that the total assets of a company available for earning profits may be enlarged by obtaining bank accommodation and credit from suppliers, rather than additional invested capital. To the extent that credit is obtained from suppliers so should an equivalent amount to pay this debt be made available as idle capital in the sum of the current assets. If extended credit is obtained, it is almost certain that the debtor will have to pay for this credit in the form of an agreed or concealed rate of interest. Bank accommodation will incur interest.

On the other hand, the British Centre for Interfirm Comparisons uses the return on total assets as their primary ratio. It may also be argued that many businesses rely largely on credit and operate on the minimum of invested capital; but these are usually the smaller type of concern. It is probable, therefore, that where external credit constitutes a large element of the funds used for profit-making purposes the return on total assets would be the appropriate measure; but for the larger business, relying heavily on invested funds, we feel that management should concentrate on the return on net assets, as representing the capital employed in the business. The more technical aspects of the assessment of capital employed are in *The Planning and Measurement of Profit* published by the Association of Certified and Corporate Accountants.

The dilemma may not be so important in practice as it appears to be academically. The essential need is for a standard rate of return, whether on total assets or net assets, to be set up in the budgetary system, and for this standard to be used as a basis for measuring the actual achievement.

THE SECOND STATISTIC: TURNOVER RATE

The turnover rate is the number of times the original capital at the beginning of a period is 'turned over' and this simply means the extent to which it is used more than once. Assuming that the percentage profit on turnover remained static, the return on capital should rise as the rate of turnover increases. Conversely, a reduction of the turnover rate below that budgeted would explain a reduction in the return on capital employed below the budgeted percentage.

It is customary to calculate the turnover rate as:

$$\frac{\text{Sales}}{\text{Capital employed}}$$

This calculation is, however, liable to give a misleading indication as to the number of times the capital in the business is 'used'. Capital is used in the purchase of goods and services. Sales are the sums which customers pay for the goods and services, and these sums may be greater or less than the capital expended in producing them, depending on the price. Thus, the only true measure of the turnover of capital is total cost, including selling and administrative expenses. The simplest method of ascertaining 'total cost' in this sense is to deduct operating profit from sales, thus eliminating financial and exceptional items from 'cost'.

EXAMPLE

Assume a business is started with a capital of £1,000 which is wholly expended in the first month in acquiring goods for sale. The business sells all the goods in the month for £1,500 and payment is received in full at the end of the month. During the month it has turned over, i.e. used its capital once:

$$\frac{(\pounds1{,}000)}{(\pounds1{,}000)} \textit{ not } 1\tfrac{1}{2} \text{ times } \frac{(\pounds1{,}500)}{(\pounds1{,}000)}$$

Assuming that the £500 profit is not withdrawn from the business, in the second month it will begin with a capital of

£1,500 which is applied to acquiring further goods for sale. It sells these goods for £2,250. The capital at the beginning of the second month has again been turned over once, not $1\frac{1}{2}$ times. Over the two months the original capital of £1,000 has been turned over:

$$\frac{£1,000+£1,500}{£1,000} = 2\tfrac{1}{2} \text{ times}$$

$$\textit{not} \; \frac{£1,500+£2,250}{£1,000} = 3\tfrac{3}{4} \text{ times}$$

THE THIRD STATISTIC: RETURN ON FIXED ASSETS*

This is a subsidiary percentage which would be appropriate to a company whose success depended largely on the efficient employment of its premises, plant and other fixed assets, as compared with one where the emphasis lay more in the marketing and stockholding areas. The essential value of this percentage to such a company is as follows:

(a) It may explain a fall below budget in the basic return on capital employed, and would suggest inefficient or inadequate usage of the equipment.

(b) If this ratio was high, but the return on capital employed was low, there would be an implication that too large a proportion of invested capital was lying idle in cash, debtors or stocks. Such a situation would be further demonstrated by reviewing the trend of the proportionate investment in (i) fixed assets and (ii) current assets.

The first sheet of the managing director's folder of financial information could appear somewhat on the lines set out below. It will be observed that so far there is no need for the manager to extract information and make his own calculations from the mass of data contained in a balance sheet and profit and loss account.

* For capital-intensive industries.

XYZ Company Limited

Financial information for the month of June 19 . .

A. Profitability of the Capital

	Budget %	Actual %
1 *Operating profit to capital employed*		
Last 12 months		
Financial year to date		
Comment:		
2 *Turnover rate*		
Last 12 months		
Comment:		
3 *Operating profit to fixed assets*		
Last 12 months		
Financial year to date		
Comment:		

Group B. Profitability of the sales

1 OPERATING PROFIT AS A PERCENTAGE OF SALES

(a) The actual percentages should be compared with budgeted percentages.

(b) Variances between budget and actual percentages will indicate one of three things:

(i) A change in volume compared with budget, thus involving a greater or less recovery of the fixed overheads.

(ii) A difference between the budgeted and actual price level. This may be caused by an opportunity to obtain higher turnover and greater profit, in the case of a fall in the price; or the need to maintain turnover by lowering price. An increase in the budgeted price level above the budget will normally be justified only where turnover is at least maintained and profit increased. A change from the budgeted price level may also be the result of a change in the sales mix of products or of customers receiving differential discounts. Any significant variance in the percentage due to price will need investigation, and if it is favourable will suggest the need to amend the next budgets.

(iii) A difference between budgeted and actual cost rates, either of the fixed or variable elements.

(c) As will appear from the foregoing, a variance in the percentage of total operating profit to total sales will provide very little positive information in itself. Thus, it is essential that the percentage be calculated and compared with the budget in respect of each of the main categories of sales.

(d) In calculating percentage profit on sales categories, it may not be possible to allocate all expenses with precision, especially those derived from the cost of administering the business as a whole. This being so, it would be better to refrain from making allocations of expenses to product groups where the allocation has no factual basis.

2 GROSS PROFIT AS A PERCENTAGE OF SALES

One of the reasons for a fall in the operating profit in relation to sales is a rise in unit costs. The operating profit is assessed after deducting from the gross profit the expenses of selling and administration, as well as other expenses not associated with the manufacturing activity. If a rise in cost is the cause of a fall in the profitability of sales, the investigation can be narrowed down to the manufacturing costs by seeing whether the gross profit percentages have fallen below budget.

3 CONTRIBUTION AS A PERCENTAGE OF SALES

The two percentages of profit on sales noted above reflect profitability *after* all normal costs, both those of a fixed and those of a variable nature, have been deducted from income. This may be described as the long-term viewpoint because it contains an implicit assumption that the fixed costs are incurred in order that the sales shall be made. It also implies that the fixed costs will rise or fall, roughly in relation to the volume of activity. This will, in fact, only be true in the long term or, more specifically, in relation to quite substantial changes in activity. Small increases in the volume of sales are unlikely to cause any noticeable increase in the building occupation costs, the depreciation of the plant or the administrative costs – unless, of course, the business is already working at the peak of capacity. Nor will there be any significant reduction in the amount of fixed expense as a result of a temporary fall in activity. It is, therefore, now necessary for the managing director's attention to be directed to the short-term aspect of sales profitability. This will be done by means of percentages representing the *contribution* in relation to sales, in total and by the major product groups, with actual percentages compared to a budget. The contribution is sales minus variable expenses. Variable expenses are those which vary in more or less direct relationship to activity. The variable expenses to be deducted from sales for this purpose will include not only those arising in the works, but also those in the selling and administrative areas. The reader should note that the contribution is quite a different concept from either gross or operating profit, and effectively represents sales, less the *additional* outgoings which the firm will incur because it has made and sold the goods.

A cost sheet setting out the contribution and, if so required, the fixed expenses allocated to a product group, would appear in the following form:

Cost Sheet

	Retail price	£
Less:	Dealer discount	———
	Realized price	£
Less:	Cost of sales (marginal)	———
	Gross margin	£
Less:	Variable expenses (selling, administration etc.)	———
	Contribution to fixed expenses and profit	£
Less:	Fixed expenses	———
	Net margin	£

The calculation of the cost of sales (marginal) involves the addition to direct works costs of an overhead rate which covers variable production costs only, and the selling and administration expenses must likewise be separated into their fixed and variable elements.

The presentation of the contribution immensely simplifies the interpretation of cost movements. If fixed and variable expenses are amalgamated, it is impossible to tell whether an increase in the total costs is due to increases in expenditure or simply to a fall in volume, causing a smaller spread of the fixed costs over the output.

4 PRICE AND VOLUME VARIANCES

The managing director will certainly want to know the figure of sales and profit in addition to percentages. The figure of sales will always be meaningful because it will be compared either consciously or subconsciously with past performance; however, a much more positive comparison will be against the budget of what it was planned that the sales total should be. This comparison needs to be made in respect of each major category of sales, and such information may give rise to a demand for further information as to sales by marketing areas and customer groups. There is no need for the managing director to waste his time examining a mass of sales statistics where no significant variance occurs between budget and actual.

Where there is a significant variance in any major category of sales it will be important for the managing director to see immediately the extent to which that variance is due to a change in price compared with the budget, as distinct from a change in volume. He will also need to follow the price and volume variances through to the gross profit figure. The calculations of the price and volume elements in a budget variance were examined in the preceding chapter.

The essential figures, as discussed above, relating to the profitability of sales may be set out in the form appended. It will be appreciated that the figures to be shown are intended merely as signposts for the purpose of isolating the areas for further inquiry and action.

B. Sales Profitability and Variances

Division—————— Period——————

Total of Product Group——————

	Total		Variances		
	Budget	Actual	Price	Volume	Total
	£	£	£	£	£
Sales:			%	%	%
Comment:					
	£	£	£	£	£
Gross profit			%	%	%
Percentage to sales	%	%			
Comment:					
	£	£	£	£	£
Operating profit					%
Percentage to sales	%	%			
Comment:					
	£	£	£	£	£
Contribution					%
Percentage to sales	%	%			
Comment:					

Group C. Efficiency of the production function

Like 'productivity', the meaning of the word 'efficiency' tends to depend on the purposes for which it is used. In the present context, efficiency means the extent to which production resources are used in the most economical manner in furthering the plans and objectives of the organization. In this sense costs will measure efficiency.

Two distinct philosophies are applied in business to the measurement of the costs of a productive operation or process. The traditional method is to attempt to record the actual expenditure incurred in carrying out an operation over a period of time or in relation to a quantity of output. If this 'historical costing' method is used, the measure of efficiency is the extent to which the 'actual' costs exceed or are less than a given standard. The standard may be assessed objectively or may simply represent past results. Amongst its other defects historical costing inevitably entails someone carrying out an elaborate exercise in comparing one figure with another before purposeful information can be presented to management.

The more effective and less time-wasting approach is to incorporate the standards into the accounting system; this is done by extracting the difference between the standard and actual costs from original documents, i.e. as close as possible in time to the point when the costs are incurred. The variances can then be recorded by each element of cost, e.g. labour, material, and overheads, and can be reported in terms of causes, e.g. variances due to price, volume and so forth.

The existence of a standard costing system has become almost essential to a sound system of financial control. It is, incidentally, equally essential to sound accounting for profit and for the valuation of stocks (which are an important ingredient of capital employed).

The gross profit shown on the preceding statements is, with a standard costing system in operation, the surplus after standard costs are deducted from sales. This is the true measure of the surplus derived from the sales before charging administrative and selling expenses. The costing variances should be deducted from the gross profit at standard to give a figure that is commonly called *gross profit, actual.* It will be observed that the costing variances do not constitute part of the cost of making the goods which have been sold. They are the cost of inefficiencies arising in the production operations for the period in question, and these production operations may well be producing goods which will be sold in a future period.

There is no need for the managing director (or, for that matter,

C. Efficiency of the Production Function

(Percentages relate to budgeted gross profit)

	Total		Works department A		B		C	
	£	%	£	%	£	%	£	%
Total costing variances								
Made up as follows:								
1 *Direct costs*								
Labour								
Rate								
Efficiency								
Total								
Material								
Price								
Usage								
Total								
Overheads								
Variable expenditure								
Fixed:								
Expenditure								
Efficiency								
Capacity								
Total fixed								
Total overheads								

Note: The above are the essential variances for the attention of general management; no doubt in some businesses the list will need extending.

any manager) to examine masses of production costs. The signposts for action for the purpose of improving efficiency are the costing variances, but since a figure in isolation is meaningless, the variances need to be brought to life by means of relationships to other figures. As they are, in effect, losses of profit which ought to have been made, they should logically be related by a percentage to the budgeted gross profit. The suggested statement covering this aspect of control is to be found on page 178.

Group D. Costs of selling and administration

For the purpose of this group, selling costs include: warehousing, distribution, sales office, selling 'in the field', advertising and publicity, and research (marketing and market research). The particular breakdown to be used will depend on what are regarded as the key factors of successful marketing in the organization concerned. Whatever breakdown is considered appropriate, it will be essential for control purposes to divide each subdivision of expense into its fixed and variable elements. In this regard *variable expenses* will cover those which can reasonably be expected to vary in relation to the volume of turnover, during the budgetary period; and, subject to the remarks in the previous chapter on the 'natural budget period', this is likely to be the past year. Fixed costs are, by inference, those which are not expected to vary during the budgetary period in relation to activity, although they will almost certainly vary in the long run.

Thus, under all subdivisions of selling costs, the fixed expenses are likely to cover the cost of the space occupied by the operation, including the lighting, heating and maintenance of the space, the depreciation of equipment and vehicles and the cost of the basic administrative effort required to maintain the operation in being, irrespective of the volume of activity. Once the fixed costs have been ascertained, the remainder can be assumed to be of a variable nature and, indeed, *must* be made variable in relation to sales. For the purposes of most effective control, the amount of costs which are accepted to be of a fixed nature, and therefore uncontrollable in the short term, should be kept to the minimum.

Administrative costs are usually regarded as largely of a fixed nature in the short term. Much depends on the organization of the administrative effort in a business. If the processing of incoming and outgoing invoices is carried out in the administrative department, and not in the buying and sales departments, then the labour and stationery involved may be considered variable.

The cost of the wages clerks may also be of a variable nature in relation to the production activity, but increasing mechanization is tending to make administrative costs uncontrollable in the short term.

What are the criteria which the managing director should adopt when examining these figures? In the case of the fixed costs the variance should be related by a percentage to budgeted operating profit, on the grounds that every adverse difference between budget and actual is so much loss of the profit which should otherwise have been achieved. If the variance percentage is small, the profit has not been significantly affected and the figures can be ignored. If the variance is a large percentage of the profit, further inquiry will be called for, and the difference will indicate one of the following: overspending on fixed overheads, increases in price or other contingencies not allowed for in the budgets.

Different considerations apply to the variable overheads. So far as the variable selling expenses are concerned, these charges can be expected to rise if the sales exceed the budget. In such

D. Selling and Administration Costs

1 *Selling costs – total*

	Budget £	% of profit	Actual £	% of profit	Variance £	% of profit
1 Fixed expenses						
	£	% of sales	£	% of sales	£	% of sales
2 Variable expenses						
	£	% of sales	£	% of sales	£	% of sales
Total						

Note: the above costs would be subdivided in a similar manner under such subheadings as: distribution, sales office, field sales force, research, advertising and publicity – as necessary.

Comments:

2 Administrative costs

	Budget £	% of profit	Actual £	% of profit	Variance £	% of profit

Comment:

circumstances, the situation will call for inquiry and action only if the variable overheads rise by a greater proportion than the rise in sales. Thus variable overheads should be related to sales, both so far as the budget and the actual figures are concerned. The managing director need be concerned only where *the percentage to sales* rises above the budgeted percentage. The suggested form of the statement is as shown on page 180 and above:

Group E. Other charges

So far, the statements will have led the managing director to review, in a logical order, the factors which have caused the difference between the operating profit budgeted and the actual operating profit achieved. There are now four other types of charges against income which must be deducted from operating profit to arrive at the final profit available for appropriation, and they are:

1 Financing expenses, e.g. interest on overdraft and loans.
2 Exceptional and non-trading items, such as book profits or losses on the disposal of fixed assets, costs, and damages arising out of a law suit.
3 Research and development, to the extent to which they are not carried forward as assets.
4 Taxation.

Financing expenses should be predictable and controllable and the budget variance does not normally have a significant effect on available profit.

The exceptional and non-trading items are very difficult to budget with accuracy and occasionally they have a large and unexpected effect on final profit. There is considerable justification for charging the more unpredictable items of this nature to a reserve account so that the picture of profitability shown by the accounts is not confused by their inclusion; although any such transfer should be referred to in the formal accounts. This is particularly applicable to capital profits and losses, which normally represent adjustments of the depreciation charged in previous periods, and are best set off against the depreciation provision.

The planning and control of research and development expenditure is considered in a subsequent chapter because of its peculiar complexity and importance to many industrial concerns. It is sufficient to say at this point that the cost may be considerable and the variance between budget and actual equally significant.

It is usual to show the balance of profit before and after taxation on the grounds that taxation is one item of unavoidable expense which is not within the control of the management (except to the extent that legal tax avoidance measures can be taken). Nevertheless, taxation must be the subject of a budget, or rather an estimate, for it will remove a very substantial proportion of the profits which would otherwise be available for the shareholders or for retention within the business. Taxation will also have a very significant effect on liquidity and the cash position.

The ony relationship which exists amongst this miscellaneous group of 'other charges' is that none of them is directly affected by the manufacturing and trading operations of the period, with the possible exception of the financing charges. To the extent that these expenses differ from the budget they will reduce the final profit, and the variances should, therefore, be shown as percentages of that figure.

It may have been observed that the traditional calculation of a percentage to sales in the case of every group of expense in the profit and loss account has not been followed in the case of costing variances, fixed expenses and the 'other charges'. The reason is that these charges do not in fact bear any relationship to sales in the short term which is under consideration. They do, however, affect the profit and their relationship to this figure should be the major concern of management.

The variances relating to the other charges should be brought to the attention of the managing director by a simple comparison between budget and actual, with the variances expressed as a percentage of the appropriate stage of profitability, in the form shown below.

E. Other charges

	£	Budget % of pre-tax profit	£	Actual % of pre-tax profit	£	Variance % of pre-tax profit
1 Financing expenses						
Comment:						
2 Non-trading items						
Comment:						
3 Research and Development						
Comment:						
4 Taxation						
Comment:						

Group F. Liquidity

The next series of statements has been deliberately entitled *liquidity* for it refers to the second major preoccupation of the managing director (after profit); that is, the provision of adequate cash to ensure that the forward plan is capable of fulfilment. This title embraces the sourcing of capital and the allocation of resources, for both these activities of management are precursors to the provision of the necessary cash balances.

An exhaustive dissection of balance sheet figures, and the ratios which may be derived from these figures, can be a fascinating exercise for an idle hour, and may well be useful for the financial analyst, but it is not normally productive of managerial action. A conclusion from such an analysis that, for example, a large proportion of the capital of an enterprise is invested in plant and machinery leads nowhere; it is putting the cart before the horse. If, on the other hand, the analyst could demonstrate that profit was below standard because of inadequate mechanization, he would have immediately pointed the way to action by management. Alternatively, the lack of sufficient cash resources to maintain the smooth flow of production and sales might be found to be due to over-investment in fixed assets. The two vital factors in the success of an enterprise are profits and cash. It is necessary for management to consider first whether these two elements are sufficient for its plans, and if they are not sufficient, to organize the resources in a manner which will remedy the deficiency. A balance sheet has been likened to a snapshot photograph of an enterprise at a moment in time: a picture of the past to put into the album. What management requires is a continuous series of future projections.

The basic projection of the future cash position is contained in the cash forecast. This accounting exercise should initially be based entirely on the system of forward budgets prepared by the management team, and it will show the likely effect on the cash position of the implementation of those plans. Clearly, it should also reflect the competence of financial management. Such competence will consist of two factors, in particular; the first is the provision of adequate funds to meet the programme and to allow for normal contingencies; the second is to ensure that there will be the minimum of idle capital. The initial cash forecast resulting from the operational plans may create a need for further temporary, medium-term or long-term capital; and if these funds cannot be provided the operational plans will have to be revised. On the other hand, the operational plans may reveal, when translated into terms of cash flow, that idle capital or surplus funds will arise. The remedies for both these contingencies will probably involve management decisions, but it is usual for the decisions to be guided by financial advice.

Once the initial cash forecast has been in operation for a month or so it will inevitably need revision. Even though sales have been maintained according to plan, there is no guarantee that customers will pay at the time expected. Forward buying of quantities larger than those scheduled in the buying programme may represent sound business tactics and will affect the cash position. Thus, even in a company where there is the closest adherence to the budgeted targets, the cash position is likely to be fluid and needs constant surveillance. Action to check periodic divergencies of cash inflow and outflow compared with expectations will be stimulated by the preparation at quarterly, or more frequent, intervals of revised cash forecasts, covering at least the next twelve months.

The cash forecast will, when compared with the actual cash position for a period, indicate the extent to which financial management has been successful in providing the funds required, and will project the future cash position. But it will not show the managing director the extent to which idle funds, which can be earning interest, are locked up unnecessarily in current assets. The current assets include: cash and bank balances, temporary investments, debtors and stocks – all of which are destined for eventual realization. It is sometimes maintained that the relationship between current assets and current liabilities should be of the order of 2:1. This is supposed to represent a healthy financial position, but it seems to us that it might indicate a distinctly unhealthy one in that an amount of the investors' capital at least equal to the sum of the current liabilities is lying idle. The reverse ratio would be more healthy if it were accompanied by a certainty that the business could meet its accruing liabilities out of future receipts from customers or, say, bank accommodation.

The ability of a business to meet its current liabilities as they become due will be demonstrated to management by a sound cash forecast. Provided that adequate funds will be forthcoming to finance the operations, the cash balances, debtors and stocks should be kept to a minimum. There is no magic standard ratio between current assets and current liabilities. The necessary amount of each current asset is capable of objective assessment by other and more valid criteria. Thus, the cash balance should ideally be no more than that necessary to pay petty cash disbursements, plus amounts in transit between branches. The standard investment in debtors will depend on the terms of credit, the extent to which customers can be persuaded to conform to those terms, and the volume of recent credit sales. Stocks of raw material, production parts and work in progress depend on the production programme, and finished goods stocks depend largely on budgeted sales (although the assessment of economic stock holding levels can be the subject of a somewhat complex exercise).

Thus, raw material stocks should represent a constant percentage of the raw material content of planned output (averaged over a period equivalent to the production cycle, say three months); work in progress should be a constant percentage of the total cost of planned output; and finished goods will represent so many days' cost of goods to be sold. Changes in the amounts of these assets compared with budgets will indicate a slowing down or speeding up of the production processes, but differences in the ratios will mean more or less idle capital than standard.

Debtors can be measured in terms of so many days' or months' recent average sales. It will probably be sufficient to show the variance on the budget in the case of cash balances and temporary investments. Work in progress should be expressed as a percentage of budgeted output (say, the average of the following three months) and the actual percentage, when compared with the budgeted percentage, will give a broad indication of whether work on the shop floor is in arrear or in advance of the programme.

The difficult question of whether expected inflation should be reflected in the forward projections is of particular importance so far as the cash forecast is concerned. That statement would become meaningless if it failed to record the certainty of increased payments due to known rises in the price of, for example, materials and labour. Such adjustments would be not so much a reflection of inflation in the form of a general rise in prices, but an allowance for known changes in the expenditure on resources, and would be a normal part of the forecasting process. Because a general rise in inflation would affect the various resources in different degrees, it would seem merely confusing to adjust current monetary figures by some overall percentage, representing the anticipated inflation index, even if that were possible to predict with reasonable accuracy. In any event the cash forecast will need revision at frequent intervals, and it should be at the time of revision when reasonably certain increases in expenditure on particular items will be taken into account. For these reasons, with the qualifications indicated above, it would be misleading to include the effect of possible future inflation in the cash forecast. Accounting, including forward accounting, is likely to lose its integrity and usefulness if it is suspected of being speculative, rather than dealing with known facts and reasonable probabilities.

A suggested form of statement for the managing director, to cover the liquidity aspect of financial control, is set out on pages 188–90.

USING THE BREAK-EVEN CHART

Some managers regard the break-even chart as merely an academic and therefore somewhat unreal device for presenting the profit plan of a business. In its simplest form, as illustrated below, the chart suggests: (a) that the fixed expenses of a business never change; (b) that variable expenses remain at a constant ratio to sales; (c) that sales remain at a constant ratio to output. Given these assumptions the profit plan can be expressed in the form of a simple mathematical model, as follows:

$S = o(p - v) - f$

Where:
S is the surplus
o is the output in units
p is the price per unit
v is the rate of variable costs per unit
f is the amount of fixed costs

F. Liquidity

1 *Cash position*

	Last year		Last quarter		Last month	
	Budget	Actual	Budget	Actual	Budget	Actual
Receipts	£	£	£	£	£	£
Trade debtors						
Others						
Capital						
Total						
Payments						
Wages						
Trade creditors						
Other operational payments						
Taxation						
Interest & dividends						
Capital						
Total						
Change in period						
Cash at beginning						
Receipts – payments						
Cash at end						

Comments:

2 *Cash Forecast*

	Mth. 1	Mth. 2	Mth. 3	Qtr. 1	Qtr. 2	Half-year	Qtr. 3	Qtr. 4	Year
Receipts	£	£	£	£	£	£	£	£	£
Trade debtors									
Others									
Capital									
Total									
Payments									
Wages									
Trade creditors									
Other operational payments									
Taxation									
Interest and dividends									
Capital									
Total									
Change in period									
Cash at beginning									
Receipts – payments									
Cash at end									

Comments:

3 *Idle funds*

(a) *Cash*	Budget £	Actual £	Variance £	% of budget

Comment:

(b) *Debtors*	Budget £	% of sales	Actual £	% of sales	Variance £	% of sales

Comment:

(c) *Raw material stock*	Budget £	Months' output	Actual £	Months' output	Variance £	Months' output

Comment:

(d) *Work in progress*	Budget £	% of output	Actual £	% of output	Variance £	% of output

Comment:

(e) *Finished stock*	Budget £	Months' sales	Actual £	Months' sales	Variance £	Months' sales

Comment:

The actual figures used in constructing the chart are:

	Sales: 100 units @ £3	= £300
Less:	Variable costs – 100 @ £1	100
	Contribution: 100 @ £2	£200
Less:	Fixed costs	150
	Surplus	£50

Whilst the assumptions remain valid it is possible to find the break-even level in terms of output or sales either by using the chart (where the break-even level of output is shown to be 75 units of output or £225 of sales) or from the formula, thus:

$O = o(3-1)-150$

Whence

$o \times 2 = 150$

$o = 75$ and sales are: $3 \times 75 = £225$

It is also possible to forecast the surplus which is likely to result from a given level of output. Thus, if the output expected to be sold is 80 units, the calculation becomes:

$S = 80(3-1)-150$

$S = 160-150 = £10$

Unfortunately, business men are only too conscious that the assumptions incorporated in the model are never completely true in practice. Sales practically never move in a straight line because (a) the incidence of orders and of output is rarely constant; (b) because prices change and may, in particular, have to be reduced to obtain additional turnover; (c) because the 'mix' of products or varieties tends to fluctuate in relation to changes in demand. Variable costs rarely move in direct relation to output and fixed costs are never absolutely 'fixed'. If these variations could be predicted with accuracy it would not be unduly difficult to incorporate their effect in the formula, at the minor expense of some complexity in the arithmetic; but if ever the time comes when

BREAK-EVEN CHART 1

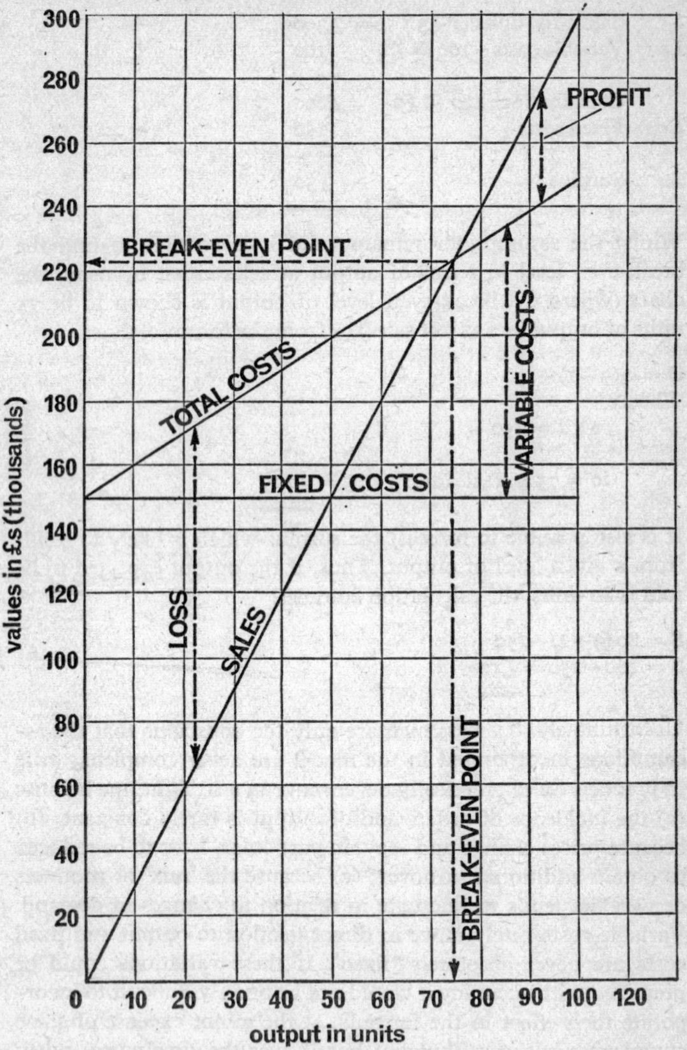

events can be accurately predicted, the role of management can be assigned to the computer. A more realistic presentation of movements in income, costs and profit might take the form of the second break-even chart.

The second chart is intended to show the position where:

(a) Sales income begins to rise steeply beyond about 20 units of output, but after 50 units the sales value per unit falls because of further turnover.
(b) After an initial rise in the rate of variable costs per unit the rise in the total costs line becomes less steep as output increases because variable costs begin to fall; but they rise again when there is pressure on productive capacity and eventually total costs are stepped upwards as further fixed facilities are brought into being.
(c) On the assumption that the utmost capacity of the works is 120 units, the chart indicates that optimum profit is reached below this level, i.e. at about 76 units of output. The implication is that the cost of the additional facilities acquired to raise output was uneconomic.

A chart of this nature can be a valuable aid to the forecasting exercise, particularly for the purpose of determining the level of output at which profits are likely to be maximized.

On the face of it, the forecasts depicted on these charts take no account of the level of capital required to finance the scale of activities shown. In theory, additional output will require additional funds to finance the necessary increase in stocks, debtors and equipment. In practice, it is often possible to increase output by using idle funds, increasing credit, speeding up collections from debtors and by temporary borrowings – up to a limit. The apparent absence of the cost of capital from the projection can, however, be overcome by including in the variable costs a notional figure representing interest on the capital which is likely to be employed at different output levels. For this purpose it is not relevant to distinguish between share capital and loan capital; nor is the actual rate of interest paid as a dividend or as interest on borrowings theoretically relevant. The rate of interest paid on ordinary shares is determined by dividend policy – some con-

BREAK-EVEN CHART 2

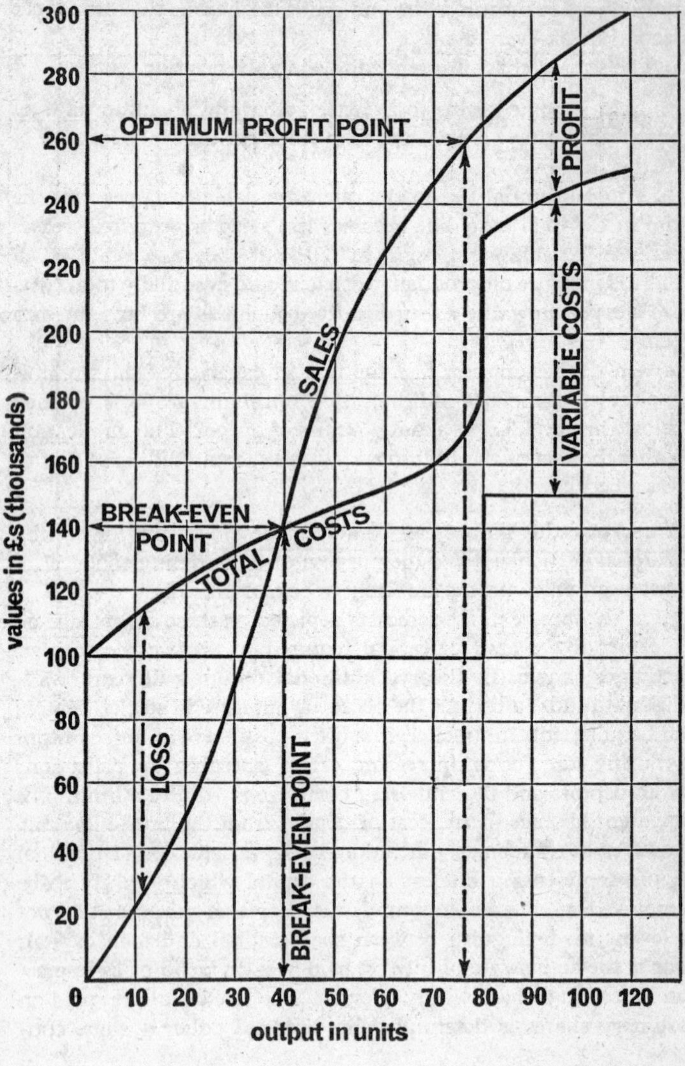

BREAK-EVEN CHART 3

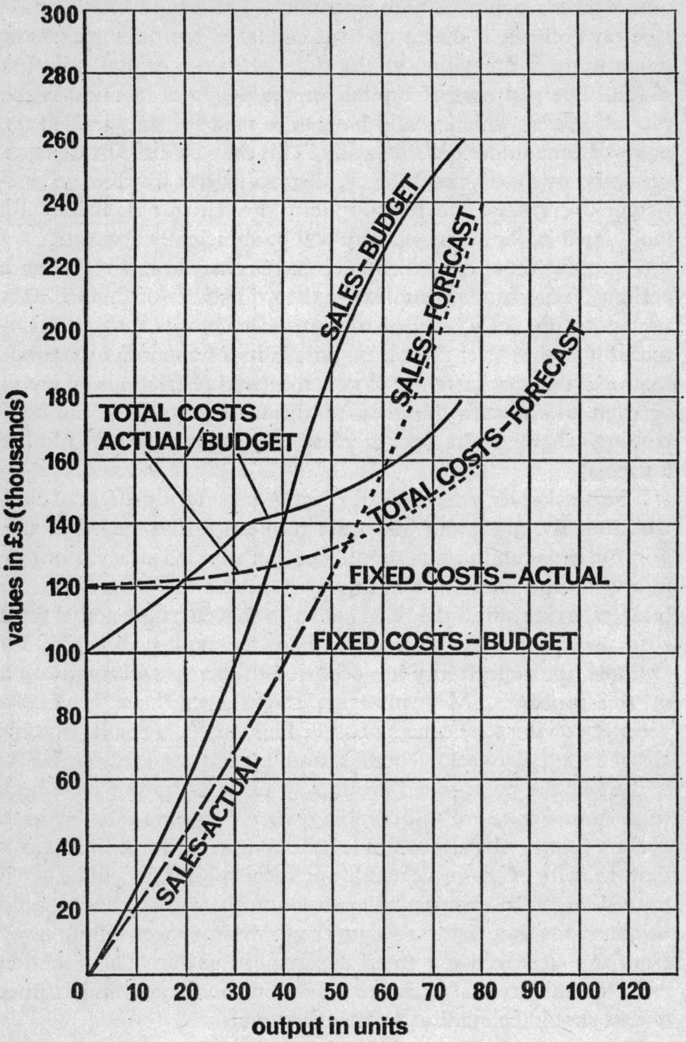

cerns pay out as dividends a high proportion of their profits, others have a policy of high retentions. The rate of interest payable on preference shares or loan capital is the outcome of the circumstances prevailing at the time when the capital was first raised. The real cost of capital for the purposes in mind is the rate of interest which would have to be paid for the funds at the point of time under consideration. This may be difficult to assess precisely, owing to the differing degrees of risk involved in particular operations, and for simplicity the return obtainable on a long-dated government security will be sufficiently accurate.

The question of capital enters into the exercise in another and, perhaps, more fundamental way; the availability of finance. It is useless to predict a level of output where profits may be maximized if at that level there is no possibility of obtaining the funds required, due, for instance, to governmental restrictions on credit or even to the unwillingness of the management or the controlling shareholders to increase the capitalization of the business.

The break-even chart has an effective use in the process of control after the plans and budgets have been formulated. For this purpose the actual results should be superimposed at, say, monthly intervals on a chart which already indicates the progress of the budgets, as set out in the third chart. In this chart the actual fixed costs are shown to be higher than the budget because, for example, the opportunity has occurred to increase mechanization of the processes. Mechanization might even have become a necessity owing to shortage of skilled labour. As a result, variable costs have fallen below budget and total costs are also below budget at the point when around 20 units of output have been sold. Actual sales are still climbing when budgeted sales begin to decline (i.e. the slope becomes less steep) and the forecast suggests that, in spite of the projected lower turnover, profit will be equal to the budget. In this particular situation the management should be conscious that there is a danger of sales turnover falling away from the steeply rising trend experienced so far. The situation calls for the greatest pressure on output and sales, and further checks should be made at frequent intervals.

Chart 3 also indicates the fairly obvious point that a business

BREAK-EVEN CHART 4

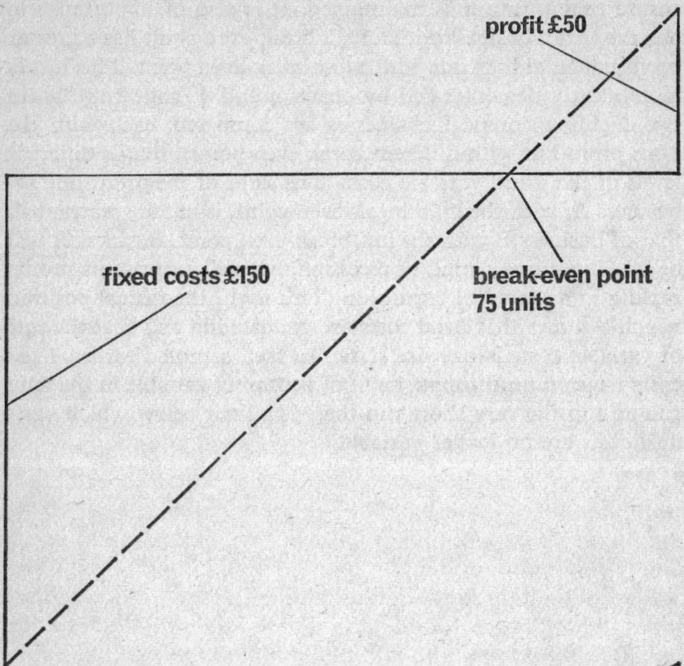

BREAK-EVEN CHART 5

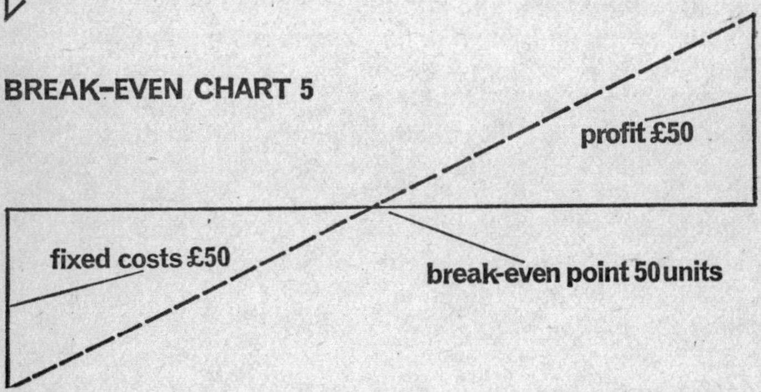

with a heavy load of fixed costs has a comparatively high break-even point, and for this reason there is an ever-present need to ensure that turnover is maintained. It is also of importance to observe that a business with a high break-even point has a greater profit potential than one with a low break-even point. This fact is more clearly demonstrated by charts 4 and 5 (page 198) where two highly theoretical businesses are compared, each with the same profit but with different break-even points, that is different levels of fixed and variable costs. The slope of the profit line for business A, with the high break-even point, is much greater than that of business B with the low break-even point. Business A will be in danger in a period of recession, but will increase its profits rapidly in a period of expansion. This is the theoretical position which assumes that fixed costs are unchanging and that the *rate* of variable costs is likewise static. In fact, as noted earlier, fixed costs have an unfortunate habit of becoming variable in the long run and in the very short run there is a limit below which variable costs are no longer variable.

9 Information for departmental managers

General considerations

Because of the great variety of businesses, and of their organizational structures, it would be extremely unwise to suggest any rigid formula for the information which departmental managers require of the accounting function. This chapter will, therefore, be confined to what is regarded as essential information, and where the suggestions which follow take a specific form they should be regarded merely as examples to be adapted to the requirements of each particular business and its managers.

In planning the information service for departmental managers, the objectives of the service must be borne in mind. It seems to us that the overall objectives are two: firstly, that the managers shall have sufficient information as to the corporate progress, and of the situation of each other's functions, that they can quickly adapt their own operations to the changing requirements of the business as a whole; second, to provide them with information which they need to plan and control their own departments in adequate detail. The first objective entails that the senior managers shall have the same, or much the same, information as is supplied to the chief executive, discussed in the preceding chapter.

The second objective involves each manager considering what information he needs and then discussing with the accountant the practicalities of producing it. The lines on which such a discussion should be conducted are that, first, the essential information should be formulated, and then consideration be given to the merits and costs of producing further detail. In too many concerns the accountant is left to decide, or takes upon himself to decide, what information the managers shall receive, with the result that many of the statements supplied represent unproductive effort and some of them may be positively misleading. The managers must be prepared to discuss their operations with the chief executive and it is their responsibility to ensure that they receive the information necessary for that purpose, as well as for their own personal requirements.

At the same time, the managers need to realize that the management accounting system of a business incurs a considerable expense which, like any other business expenditure, is justified only if it helps to produce income, however indirectly. A business has a choice between spending money on accounting personnel, machinery and systems or, for example, increasing advertising or acquiring further productive machinery. It is not easy to quantify the benefits of any form of information service, but it is not so difficult to ensure that it does not incur expense in producing unwanted statistics which waste the time of a large number of people. Thus, a manager cannot expect to receive financial information on every conceivable problem that *might* arise. The system must produce the essential information as a matter of routine, but should also incorporate sufficient flexibility for special investigations to be carried out as and when a real need arises.

The timing and frequency of the information will require careful consideration. Where action can be taken quickly the information may need to be supplied at weekly intervals, and sometimes daily. This would apply, for instance, to information on labour efficiency, material usage and machine utilization; and sometimes to the sales of a newly launched product. Experience suggests that managers rarely have time to digest anything but 'crisis reports' at less than monthly intervals. It is, in this connection, a good plan for a manager to allocate a specific day and time each month for the perusal of the last month's results; and for this purpose it is essential that the information shall be provided for him regularly by the appointed date.

Where it is known that only minor variations from the normal occur, it may be quite sufficient for quarterly or half-yearly reports to be submitted. The review of operating results has some analogies with the routine checks which require to be made to motor cars; it is only the parts which tend to break down frequently which require regular servicing.

We consider below some examples of the more essential information which will be required as a matter of routine in a manufacturing business. Clearly, these examples will need amendment and development according to the needs and circumstances of each business.

The sales manager's requirements

(1) *Invoiced sales and their contributions*

On the grounds that the sales manager is not only responsible for getting orders but also, as a member of the management team, for ensuring that, so far as lies within his power, the sales produce the planned profit, we suggest that the first matter to which his attention should be directed is the sales (i.e. deliveries) made in a period and the contribution to company profit derived from those sales. An inadequate contribution might be remedied:

(a) by improving the 'mix', i.e. putting more effort on those products which produce a larger contribution per unit of the limiting factor;
(b) by price changes; or
(c) simply by increasing volume overall.

The remedies for inadequate profitability in relation to the plan would be indicated by a statement on the lines (simplified) set out in figure 1 (page 202). This statement refers to three product groups only, but in most businesses a much more numerous breakdown would be necessary. The period covered by the statement would normally be a month or a four-weekly period, but where a product line needed closer surveillance a more frequent presentation might become essential for control purposes. For the purpose of examining the longer-term position of sales, an additional statement showing the cumulative total for the past year should be prepared. From the sales manager's point of view we see no great merit in presenting a statement of the cumulative for the year to date, for that approach will be adequately dealt with in the information provided for the chief executive.

It will be observed that the form of statement outlined in figure 2 (page 203) is designed to concentrate the manager's attention on a single point – the extent to which the actual results have conformed to the results planned and budgeted, but the statement should be presented both on a short-term (e.g. monthly) and a medium-term (annual) basis. There should be no question, for the purposes in mind, of diverting the manager's attention to the question of whether the sales and contributions are rising or falling, or the rate of increase or decrease in the figures; those aspects are important for the purpose of preparing or revising the budgets but are quite irrelevant for the purpose of controlling operations to achieve the budgets once they have been established.

Nor is there any advantage, for control purposes, in presenting the sales manager with figures showing the net profitability of the different lines of sales, after making the conventional accounting allocations and apportionments of fixed expenses. This is not to

Sales analysis
figure 1

Department __________ *Period* __________

Product group	SALES		VARIANCE			% of budget
	Budget	Actual	Price	Volume	Total	
A						
B						
C						
TOTAL						

Contribution analysis
figure 2

Product group	CONTRIBUTION Budget	Actual	VARIANCE Price	Volume	Total	% of budget
A per hour						
B per hour						
C per hour						
TOTAL per hour						

say that the calculation of the 'net' profit of a product line is an entirely useless piece of information. What such information does indicate – and only indicate – is the long-term profitability of a product line, and is based on the assumption that if the facilities represented by the fixed costs were not applied to the production and sale of the product, they could be applied for some other profit-earning purpose *in the long term*. For this reason, statements of net profit, after making rational allocations and apportionments of fixed costs, would be useful for long-term planning purposes, but not in controlling operations in the short and medium term. For the latter purposes, the crucial factor is the optimum application of the limited resources available which, for practical purposes, can be reduced to a consideration of the contribution per unit of the limiting factor, normally hours of work.

(2) *Departmental expenses*

The second important area to which the sales manager's attention should be directed covers the control of his departmental expenses. Once again, the presentation should be concentrated on the simple point of a comparison between the budget and the actual costs. In the short term, some of the departmental expenses will be static in relation to selling activity – the so-called fixed costs – and the variances will indicate either excess spending or that the original budgets contained errors. Excess spending may, of course, be due to uncontrollable external circumstances (which should be noted) or to inefficiency in the control of the costs.

The control of the variable costs requires, however, a somewhat different approach. A straight comparison between budget and actual in respect of these costs is inadequate and can be misleading. Where variable costs exceed the budget, the excess may be due to the achievement of higher turnover than expected; likewise, where the turnover is below that budgeted the variable expenses should, in theory, bc correspondingly below the budgeted figures. The important statistic, then, so far as the variable expenses are concerned, is the percentage they bear to turnover compared with the budgeted percentage; the difference between these percentages needs explanation and should be the subject of control action.

Although in the ultimate it is the relationship between income and costs which is important in achieving profitability, nevertheless it may be desirable, for the purpose of explaining significant variances between budgeted and actual variable cost percentages, to calculate some more direct relationships. Thus, the cost of processing orders, inquiries, and invoices, is appropriately related to the number of documents dealt with; in this way it might be demonstrated that a rise in the rate of variable costs in the sales office is due to an increase in the number of small orders being accepted, and this information might lead to a simplification of the system or, possibly, the imposition of a surcharge on small orders. The cost of stocking may be related to the number of items carried in stock, or their weight or size. Salesmen's commission can, assuming it is on a differential basis (i.e. reducing in rate as sales rise), be related to the contribution obtained from the sales concerned, since there is no point in paying commission at all if it brings the contribution of the marginal sales below an economic level.

Some of the sales expenses, such as advertising and market research, may be considered as of a variable nature, but they are designed to produce future income, and there is no point in relating them to current sales. In such cases a straight comparison between budget and actual is appropriate as presumably the budget has been established in relation to the income which these expenses are designed to produce.

The manager should not have his time wasted and his attention distracted by an accumulation of small amounts. Usually the most significant picture of departmental expenses is presented by grouping expenses by functional headings in the lines set out in figure 3 (page 206). For example, the cost of the field force would include commission and travelling and entertaining expenses. Communications would include telephone calls, postage, telex messages, cables, and stationery. Under fixed expenses, personnel costs would cover salaries, national insurance and subscriptions payable by the company. Building occupation costs cover rent, rates, heating, lighting, and maintenance.

For the sake of conformity with the statement of invoiced sales and contributions, the departmental expense statement should be presented in two parts: one showing figures for the previous month and the other for the previous year. The longer the period covered by the figures so the fixed costs move progressively into the variable category. Thus, within a period of a year the salary bill (which is an essentially fixed charge over a month or so) can be adapted to the level of activity, either by means of natural wastage of staff or further recruitment, as the need arises. For this reason *all* the figures for the yearly period should be related by percentages to sales, and with these figures it will be the variances of the percentages which become of importance.

A specimen statement is set out in figure 3.

Departmental expenses

figure 3

Department ________________ *Period* ________________

Expense group	Budget	% of sales	Actual	% of sales	Variance	% of budget
1 *Variable*						
Field force						
Communications						
Packaging						
Carriage						
Insurance						
Travelling and entertaining						
Other variable expenses						
Total variable						
2 *Fixed*						
Personnel						
Building occupation						
Depreciation						
Management and supervision						
Other fixed expenses						
Total fixed						
3 *Long term*						
Market research						
Publicity						
Total long term						
GRAND TOTAL						

(3) *Capital expenditure*

This statement needs little comment, except to note that whilst some companies adopt fairly rigorous procedures for the submission and approval of capital projects, less effort is exerted in checking the extent to which the approvals are properly implemented or whether the actual expenditure exceeds the approvals. The subject was considered at some length in chapter 6. It is just as important for a manager to control his capital spending as his income and expenditure on revenue account. A simple form of statement, containing ample room for explanations, is suggested in figure 4 below. It would normally be quite sufficient for such a statement to be prepared at quarterly intervals.

figure 4

Capital expenditure

Department ______ *Period* ______

Type of expenditure	Budgeted cost	Authorization ref.	date	Actual cost	Orders placed
Totals					

Comments:

(4) *The 'order book'*

So far, the information suggested represents the final outcome of the sales manager's work, in terms of delivered sales, capital and revenue expenditure, and contributions to profit. He should now consider how the intake of orders, and the balance of orders awaiting delivery, is likely to affect the future results.

It will be important to watch the trend of the order intake for two reasons: firstly, as an indication of where action is needed to reinforce the efforts of the field force (e.g. by publicity, strengthening numbers, changing discount structure); secondly, to act as a guide where a revision of future budgets is necessary. Trends are usually best depicted in the form of a simple graph or chart. Where the order intake usually fluctuates widely month by month the trend may be difficult to determine if the actual monthly totals are charted, but will be seen more clearly if a moving total or moving average is used.

Thus, a moving annual total chart can be constructed from the total of twelve months' sales to each month end. Those figures can be converted into a twelve months' moving average by dividing each twelve months' total by twelve. A six-monthly or even three-monthly moving average is frequently found useful for charting orders receivable, which are susceptible to short-term fluctuations by reason of changes in taste, competitors' activities, and advertising effectiveness.

Having considered the trend of the order intake, it is now desirable that the sales manager shall direct his attention to the balance of orders outstanding. The importance of this figure is not so much in the absolute amount, or even whether it shows a rising or falling trend, but in the delivery delay which it implies. Whilst a growing order book is usually regarded with some satisfaction, it may in fact indicate lengthening delivery dates with consequent loss of customer goodwill and possible cancellations. On the other hand, if production is expanding it is quite possible for a rising total of outstanding orders to be accompanied by a shortening of delivery delays.

Thus it is important that the balance of orders outstanding be represented as so many days', weeks', or months' output, by using for this purpose not the past or current rate of output, but the budgeted rate in the near future. Since there are few manufacturing concerns where both the output and the outstanding orders can be expressed in terms of standard articles, it will usually be necessary to convert the orders into terms of man hours of work or some such measure common to both sales and output.

The figure showing the number of weeks' or months' production represented by the outstanding orders will be a useful statistic to both the sales manager and the production manager, and the production manager should therefore also be supplied with a copy of the statement. Whilst both functional managers will be aiming to achieve the budgeted activity, there will be inevitable variations between actual results and planned results, at least in the short term. Assuming that some flexibility exists, as it should do, the statistic will be a guide to the production manager in doing what he can to adjust output to short-term changes in demand; and it will be a guide to the sales manager in adjusting the intake of orders to plant capacity. In a highly automated concern the rate of output is less amenable to short-term adjustment so that in this situation the emphasis lies in tailoring the intake to the output; in other types of production, such as work of a jobbing nature where orders have to conform to customers' specifications, there is a need for the greater flexibility to lie in the production function.

Even in an automated plant, the effect of relative inflexibility in the rate of production can be minimized by permitting temporary fluctuations in stock levels. The situation would need careful reappraisal where a tendency developed for stocks to fall considerably below, or rise considerably above, economic levels. For this reason the sales manager's attention must next be drawn to movements in finished stocks.

A simple form of statement showing the outstanding order position is set out in figure 5 (page 210). In some situations it may be considered desirable to insert columns showing budgets, but we feel that such a complication of the statement might distract attention from its essential purposes – to indicate the time which will be involved in producing the goods or services. In a complex business the statement will need breaking down, as appropriate, by divisions, product groups, customer classes, and geographical areas. It is perhaps advisable at this point to mention that the object of this, and the other statements outlined in this chapter, is to give an indication of the 'total position' to the managers concerned; it is presumed that progress clerks are controlling deliveries from works and dispatch departments of individual orders.

figure 5

Orders received and outstanding

Month		*Group*		
		Products		
	A £	B £	C £	Total £
Orders in hand at beginning of month				
Orders received in month				
Total	£			
Orders delivered in the month				
Orders cancelled				
Total	£			
Orders in hand at end of month	£			
Representing:				
Month's output				

(5) *The stock position*

The purpose of the preceding statement was to indicate the extent to which the intake of orders was in balance with the output of goods. The sales manager's next concern should be to consider whether the levels of finished goods stocks are adequate from the sales point of view. The sales viewpoint will not normally be decisive in determining whether stocks are adequate because the economic stock levels will also be influenced by the amount of idle capital which the business can afford to leave invested in stocks. In essence, the assessment of what is an economic stock level is an investment decision. The calculation should depend, in theory at least, on a calculation as to whether an investment of x amount in stocks will result in a greater return than an investment of y amount, taking into account interest on the different capital sums involved. In practice, a great deal will depend on the question of whether a certain level of stocks will result in a delivery period to customers which will maintain goodwill, i.e. repeat orders. Thus, from the sales manager's viewpoint the importance of watching stock levels lies not in their absolute amounts but in the delivery periods to customers which they represent.

Stock levels should, accordingly, be related to budgeted future sales and the clearest picture is usually obtained by expressing stocks as so many days', weeks', or months' sales. Since stocks will be valued normally at production cost they must be related, not to budgeted sales revenue, but to the *cost* of future sales.

A form of statement, which will show the recent trend in finished stock levels, is set out in figure 6 (page 212). Actual and budgeted amounts are included in the statement on the grounds that it is desirable that the sales manager appreciates the amount of money invested in each major stock category, but the essential statistic is the number of weeks' sales which the stocks represent, compared with the budgeted figure. For stock of a uniform character it may also be desirable to show quantities.

Where the number of weeks' sales in stocks is high or tending to rise, the first matter for consideration is whether sales can be stimulated. The remedy of reducing the rate of output is less attractive because such action normally entails the cost of switching productive facilities to another activity or, if this is not practicable, creating idle capacity. Where an adverse trend of this nature has been allowed to continue uncontrolled for a considerable period the immediate action required may be to dispose of excess stock at a loss or reduced price in order to eliminate running costs in space and the administrative effort caused by the presence of the redundant stock. In order to guard against the need to take such drastic action, the sales manager should next consider a statement showing an analysis of the stock by age. Depending on the nature of the demand, any tendency for stock to move into the longer age groups calls for immediate investigation and action. One of the most frequent and insidious

figure 6

Finished goods stocks

Month end												B = budget A = actual
	This month				Last month				Preceding month			
	Amount		Weeks' sales		Amount		Weeks' sales		Amount		Weeks' sales	
	B £	A £	B	A	B £	A £	B	A	B £	A £	B	A
Product category												
1												
2												
3												
4												

causes of failure in business is the concealed presence of redundant stock which will not realize its recorded values.

A form of statement showing the ageing of stock is provided in figure 7 (page 213).

Finally, on this subject, we would recommend the desirability of sales departments being responsible for the finished goods' store and the maintenance of economic stock levels, as otherwise that department will have a natural tendency to encourage over-stocking.

figure 7
Stock ages
Month end

	Ages in months						
Product category	Under 1	1–2	2–3	3–6	6–12	Over 12	Total
1							
2							
3							
4							
Total							

The production manager's requirements

(1) *General considerations*

The production manager's essential responsibility is to produce the goods and services required in accordance with the plan. This assumes that the company will have drawn up plans which coordinate all activities and set out the required volume, quality, and cost of production. If the simple philosophy stated above is accepted it means that the job of the production department is not merely to satisfy the demands of the selling function, which are likely to vary with the inevitable changes which occur in demand, competition, and external circumstances, but to satisfy the demands of the plan. Nevertheless, it is a truism of business that budgets, however carefully drawn up, are often overtaken by events, and a need arises for a business to make short-term changes in the details of a planned programme. For this reason the production department must be prepared to cope with minor unforeseen variations in activities and will need to cooperate with the sales departments in particular for this purpose. The financial information required by the production manager will, therefore, be basically a comparison between his actual performance and the budgets, but he will also require information, which will guide him in meeting unpredicted changes in requirements.

Much of the information requirements of the production manager will be quantitative rather than monetary, but quantitative data has financial implications. The following notes concentrate on the basic information which affects financial control in the production department.

(2) *Finished output*

Just as the sales manager's main preoccupation should be to de-

figure 8
Finished output
Period

	Budgets			Actual			Variances		
	£	Hours	Units	£	Hours	Units	£	Hours	Units
Product groups									
1									
2									
3									
4									
Totals									

liver goods to customers, so the production manager should direct his energies to delivering finished work into finished goods stores in accordance with the agreed plans or budgets. The first statement is, therefore, a comparison between actual and budgeted completed output in terms of quantities and value. In some cases it may be possible and of value to record the number of units produced in a period, but where the units are not standard a broadly applicable measure, such as man hours, machine hours, or operating hours, will have to be used to measure volume. The man hours etc. to be used for this purpose should be standard times, for the use of actual times which are inflated by inefficiencies might indicate that the budgeted output is being achieved when in fact the actual volume of goods going into stores is below the planned quantities. In other words, the standard times used for budgeting purposes can be validly set off against standard times of actual output, and the variances recorded as inefficiencies or above normal efficiency.

Figure 8 opposite shows the basic form of statement required. This form will no doubt require considerable adaptation to meet the particular needs of each individual production department.

A similar form would show the cumulative figures for the past twelve months or other appropriate medium-term period. The variances should be expressed as percentages of budget as well as absolute amounts.

(3) *Production profitability*

Increasing use is being made in industry of interdivisional pricing between production and sales departments, and this system involves the assumption that the production department sells its output to the sales department at a given profit on standard costs. The percentage to be used is most scientifically calculated as a reasonable return on the capital employed in the production department, say 10%; if the production department turns its capital over twice in a year, it will then be allowed a notional profit of 5% on standard costs. The precise percentage used is immaterial. The resulting profit or loss shown by the production department is a broad measure of its efficiency, for the budgeted profit will be reduced by adverse variances on standard costs and by output which is below the budgeted volume. In some cases the production department is permitted to obtain orders, usually subcontract work, from external sources, particularly when the sales department is unable to utilize capacity. In other cases a price for each order is negotiated with the sales department on the basis of what would have to be paid to an outside supplier. The latter device can be very difficult to operate and often results in quite unproductive argument and even dissension, thus destroying the vital spirit of cooperation which should exist between the two functions.

If the system outlined above is in operation, the production manager should be supplied with a profit and loss statement on the lines indicated in figure 9 (page 217).

(4) *Standard cost variances*

The total variances are shown in the production profit and loss account described above. These total figures will, however, be aggregates of the various variances arising in different production shops, cost centres, and operations. It is unlikely that the variances can realistically be applied to products, except by a process of arbitrary apportionment which tends merely to confuse the issue. Thus, the production manager will require a statement of variances for each major cost centre, and it is essential, if prompt remedial action is to be taken, that the statement be issued at frequent intervals and be up to date. It is assumed that more detailed statements, relating to works orders, batches, and contracts, will be supplied to superintendents and foremen at appropriate stages in the progress of each order. The precise nature of the variances to be analysed by the cost section will depend on the requirements of each particular business, but figure 10 (page 219) is an illustration of the basic form suitable to a manufacturing concern.

Note: in order to watch the trend of efficiency in the works cost centres the production manager will probably find it useful to keep a simple weekly graph of the percentage variances.

figure 9

Production department – profit and loss account

Period ______________________

	Current month	Year to date
Finished output in units		
At transfer price	£	£
Less: Standard costs		
Departmental profit at standard	£	£
Less: Cost variances –		
Labour rate		
Labour efficiency		
Material price		
Material usage		
Variable overhead: expenditure		
Fixed overheads: expenditure		
capacity		
efficiency		
Total variances	£	£
Departmental profit/loss – ——actual——	£	£

(5) *Departmental overhead expenses*

The production manager will need regular information to aid him in controlling the overhead expenses of his departments. It is important that production overheads be divided into the fixed and variable categories. The fixed overheads should not vary in the short term and this control should be directed at ensuring that they conform to the budgets. Since the question whether some expenses are of a fixed or variable nature can only be solved by an arbitrary decision, it will also be desirable to relate fixed overheads to the volume of output (usually the volume of output is best measured in terms of *standard* hours of work performed). So far as the really long-term overheads are concerned, however, a rise in the cost per unit of output may be the result of falling production rather than excessive overhead cost.

Unless output is stable and shows little variation from month to month in relation to budgets, a comparison between budgeted and actual variable overheads is of little use for control purposes. The reason is that a rise in output will justify, and even necessitate, an increase in indirect labour and indirect material costs, and vice versa. Thus, so far as variable overheads are concerned, the production manager's attention should be directed towards a comparison between budgeted and actual variable overhead rates per unit of output.

Because of the somewhat different approach which is suggested in the foregoing with regard to the control of (a) fixed and (b) variable overheads, it is desirable that, where there is some doubt as to the variable nature of the expense, it should be placed in the fixed category. In this way it will tend to be controlled in relation to the budget in the short term but in relation to output in the long term. Because in the long term it is necessary that the total of production overheads shall be controlled in relation to output, it is necessary that both fixed and variable overheads be combined in one statement so that the total is expressed as a rate per man hour or other applicable measure of production activity.

A form of statement incorporating the features mentioned above is given in figure 11 (page 220).

In order that the production manager shall be able to trace the responsibility for adverse variances, he will need to be supplied with similar statements showing the results achieved by each of the departments controlled by his subordinate managers, and this will apply to both direct production shops and to service departments. In all cases the statements should be in two parts, one covering the results of the current month and the other cumulative results for the year to date.

figure 10
Standard cost variances

	Week							
Cost centre	A		B		C		Total	
	£	%	£	%	£	%	£	%
Variance								
Labour								
– rate								
– efficiency								
Total labour								
Material								
– price								
– usage								
Total material								
Variable overhead								
– expenditure								
Fixed overheads								
– expenditure								
– capacity								
– efficiency								
Total overheads								
Grand total								

Comments:

figure 11

Production department overheads

Period *Output in standard man hours:*

Budget:
Actual:

	Budget £	per hour	Actual £	per hour	Variance £	%	per hour
Variable overheads							
Indirect labour							
Indirect materials							
Communications							
Consumable tools							
Maintenance							
Sundry variable expenses							
Total variable							
Fixed overheads							
Management							
Supervision							
Clerical							
Building occupation							
Depreciation							
Hiring charges							
Other fixed expenses							
Total fixed							
Grand total							

It is important to observe that the allocation and apportionments to departments made by the accounting department for costing purposes do not apply to these statements. The ultimate object of costing is to arrive at a cost per job and per product, and frequently this is a largely notional figure which depends on its underlying assumptions. The object of the statements under discussion is to aid in the planning and controlling function and this entails that the activity and expense attributed to a manager shall only be that over which he exercises a measure of direct control.

(6) *Capital expenditure*

The form of statement will be similar to that applicable to the sales department and illustrated by figure 4 (page 207).

(7) *Works order book*

The form of statement will, again, be similar to that illustrated in figure 5 (page 210) for the sales department. In the case of works orders, however, the orders should be expressed in some overall measure of capacity utilization, such as standard hours of work, and no purpose is served by converting them into value.

It will be apparent, at this stage, that both of the major areas of business activity – producing goods and services and selling them – are treated as of the nature of distinct businesses, and thus the basic information provided to the respective managers has many similarities.

(8) *The stock position*

Production stocks fall into the two broad divisions of (a) materials and (b) work in progress. Materials may be further subdivided, according to the needs of the business, into raw materials, parts for production, and components bought out.

The production manager needs to exercise a close watch on materials stock levels because shortages will delay production and excess stocks mean loss of interest on capital and probably stock losses. It is, therefore, important that economic stock levels are budgeted in relation to the volume and characteristics of the planned production. The stocks should be compared to budgets in quantities and value and should be expressed as so many days' or months' production requirements.

The form of the statements illustrated in figures 6 and 7 (pages 212 and 213) for finished goods can be adapted for the purpose of showing whether the required levels of production stocks are being maintained.

(9) *Other statistics*

The foregoing are suggested as representing the essential statements for aiding the financial control of the production function. Depending on circumstances, the production manager will from time to time require a good deal of statistical information, much of it of a financial nature. He will, for example, require information with regard to the usage of machine capacity, the rate of rejects and the economics of replacing various articles of plant. What is important is that he does not encumber himself with the need to examine a vast mass of information month by month and thus take his sights off the main target. He should call for additional information only when he requires it, and avoid the chronic disease of operating managers which tends to turn them into subsidiary accountants and statisticians.

In a book of this nature, it is clearly impossible to set out a system of reporting applicable to every kind of business, or even for a range of businesses. It is for this reason that a manufacturing concern has been used for the sake of illustration. If, however, in another type of industry the centre of direct operations is put in the place of the workshop, the principles inherent in the above description of a financial information service have equal application. The forms will, of course, need considerable adaptation; but in every business the situation exists of the direct operating department receiving orders from the selling function and requiring information as to the efficiency with which those orders are processed and fulfilled.

Information for administrative departments

It is probable that the widest variety of business functions are to be found in what are simply termed here 'the administrative departments' of industry and commerce. These are essentially the departments which provide a service to the major operating departments or to general management. This category will certainly include an accounts department, probably subdivided into financial accounts, budgets, costs, wages and salaries; it will probably embrace the personnel department, comprising employment, training, welfare, and labour relations; there may be a computer with programmers, input processors, operators, and an output analysing section; a general office may include a filing section, mailing, typing, and a messenger service.

The financial information requirements of the managers of these departments are traditionally concentrated on the surveillance of departmental costs, but the watching of costs *per se* can be an unrewarding exercise, and may even be misleading, unless the expenditure is related to a measure of activity. Each administrative department should be regarded as another workshop responsible for achieving the planned volume of work at an economic level of expense per unit of activity produced. The economic cost per unit of activity emerges as a result of experience and a study of future needs, allied to continuous efforts to improve efficiency; this is the basis of the departmental budget against which results should be compared.

As in the production and sales departments, the essence of the control should be to ensure that variable expenses remain at the budgeted level, *when expressed as a cost per unit of activity.* The fixed departmental costs should be controlled in relation to the budgeted *amount* in the short term, but will also have to be controlled in relation to activity in the long term.

The major difficulty in controlling costs in the administrative departments on the lines suggested above is to decide on an effective measure of activity for each department. In the long term it may be said that administrative costs must be related to the volume of output, expressed in quantities of a standard product or in standard productive hours where the output is not homogeneous. But relating administrative cost to output is a matter for long-term budgeting and is of little use to the manager who requires a day-to-day measure; especially when the activity of his department in the short term may bear little relation to current rates of output. Nevertheless, in the absence of a measure of departmental activity, cost control becomes a matter of guesswork.

The answer to the problems appears to lie in the creation of 'cost centres' in the administrative departments so that each such centre has a recognizable activity factor. Thus, the cost of the personnel, wages and salaries departments should relate to the number of employees' services; the cost of the 'receivables' and 'payables' ledger sections to the numbers of invoices processed; likewise, the work of the machine accounting, typing, filing, and manning sections is susceptible to counting and even mechanical metering in some cases.

These detailed measures are for the supervisors of the cost centres. For the statements issued to the superior managers, such as the chief accountant and office manager, who are more concerned with the longer-term picture, costs will have to be related to the appropriate factor of production output.

Information for the Research and Development Department

It has become customary to regard research and development as not being susceptible to precise budgeting and that, consequently, the costs of the activity are incapable of control by means of budgets. Likewise, it is debatable whether the current costs of research and development can be properly related to any known measure of activity because the efforts of the department, some of which will prove abortive, are designed to produce future products and future services.

Nevertheless, whatever basis is used, it is necessary that budgets, both of activity and expense, shall be formulated for the research and development department otherwise the people engaged in that department will suffer no constraints – or merely pettifogging ones – on either costs or periods in which projects are to be completed. This is a profit-earning department the same as any other and the justification for its existence can lie only in the extent to which the income which it produces is greater than the cost incurred (including, incidentally, interest on the capital involved in the function).

The costs incurred by the department will be (a) direct costs, i.e. those incurred directly on project work, and (b) indirect costs or overheads, i.e. those which cannot be ascribed with precision to particular projects, including general administration of the department, supervision, and all forms of idle time.

Dealing first with direct work on projects, it is important that the budgets contain two essentials (whatever may be the degree of intelligent guesswork involved): first, monthly figures of permitted cost against each project, and second, a time period in which the project should be completed. The first requirement is often not so difficult to achieve as may appear on the face of the problem, since it is usual for a team to be assigned more or less continuously to a project, and at least the cost of that team will be capable of reasonably precise assessment. The second requirement requires greater powers of foresight – or, perhaps, greater talents for control – and it will almost certainly require amendment from time to time. Since, however, costs move largely in relation to time, the absence of an estimated completion date means complete lack of cost control.

In reporting R and D costs to departmental management it is insufficient merely to compare actual expenditure against the budgets; because the work may have proceeded more or less quickly than was anticipated in the budgets. A statistic as important as past costs is an estimate of costs to come; and in this respect the control of R and D costs is comparable to the control of costs on a major contract. Clearly, the estimate of costs to come must come from the technical people, not from the accountant, and will depend largely on whether any further time or less time is required for completion than was at first planned. Once technical management can be persuaded to make the initial estimates, experience suggests that they become increasingly interested in developing expertise at cautious prediction and flexible control of the effort. Non-technical managers are too prone to assume that their technical colleagues are not interested in efficiency and profitability; what is necessary is that the latter shall be *involved* in these aspects of business.

A simple form of statement incorporating the suggestions outlined above is shown by figures 12 (overleaf) and 13 (page 227).

figure 12

Research and development projects

Expenditure for the month of ______________________

Project no.	Budget	Actual costs	Variance	
	£	£	£	%
10				
12				
15				
16				
17				
etc				
Total				

The reporting of the research and development department's indirect costs or overheads will follow the same lines as the reporting of the overheads of the production department. All figures should be compared with budgets and the statement should be divided into the fixed and variable overhead categories. Both categories of expenses should be related to the activity of the department and this activity will be best measured as so many direct man hours booked to projects. Once again, we would emphasize that the statement should exclude apportionments of the costs of other departments, such as accounts, security, canteen, which may provide services to the R and D department. It is the job of the accountant, the security officer, and the canteen manageress to control their own costs, in relation to the services which they are required to provide. Likewise, if the R and D department provides services to, say, the production department

figure 13
Research and development projects
Expenditure to date and estimates to completion

Month:

Project no.	Labour	Material	Sub-contract	Equipment	Total actual	Budget
	£	£	£	£	£	£
10						
Costs to date						
Costs to come						
Costs to completion						
Budget to completion						
Estimated variance						
	and so on for other current projects					

it is quite illogical to assume, for control purposes, that the costs attributable to the R and D department are to that extent reduced. It might, of course, be desirable for the job costing system to record such apportionments; but that is another purpose for the figures.

10 The problem of the future

To those managers who can scarcely find time to deal with the problems of today, one of the more annoying axioms of the theorists is that they must continually be planning for the future. Nevertheless, few managers would deny the truth of the latter statement. In this book the manager's task is identified as not confined to mere prediction, but consisting of the essential functions of forward planning, comparing performance with plans, control and replanning; these exercises must ultimately be expressed in monetary terms. The businessman is not expected to perform the miracle of controlling future events but to ensure, so far as he can, that his business is continually adapted to change.

The task will be easier if the range of possible change can be foreseen, at least in part. The difficulty is the traumatic rapidity with which changes have occurred even during the past few decades. New laws, new technology, changes in the nature of society, in markets and people's tastes and fancies rush past in an impressionistic blur of words and events. If the businessman attempts a study in depth of all these changes he will assuredly neglect his business; if he fails to detect what is relevant he may find that his affairs have been overtaken by events.

It would be presumptuous to suggest that there is an easy answer to the conflicting demands of the present and the future, or between the need for action and the need for study. What is important is that managers maintain at least an awareness of the major trends and tendencies likely to affect business, and concentrate on those which seem most apposite to their own concerns. An attempt is made in this chapter to indicate some of those trends and tendencies.

The nature of change

To delineate the nature of the major changes likely to affect the business, it seems logical first to attempt a brief examination of underlying causes. Superficially it may be said that business will be affected by the developments which are occurring in technology, the structure of society and of its political organizations, the growth of competition, and communications on a worldwide front. But what has caused these developments? Are they ultimately due to man's insatiable desires and his acquisitive nature? A further factor is surely the innate mental restlessness of man, his need for change for the sake of change, and his inherent curiosity.

The environment in which a business operates may therefore change (a) as a result of some logical and consequently predictable development, and (b) from some 'cause ill defined' and which is not capable of prediction. The conclusion is hardly startling and accords with experience, as most businessmen can confirm, probably giving emphasis to the latter category. What it means from a practical point of view is that all businesses, from the small village shop to the international combine, must have sufficient flexibility to cope with the unforeseeable. It means also that both kinds of enterprise *should* prepare for the possible and *must* prepare for the probable.

Technological change will affect the raw materials from which the product is made, the methods and machinery of manufacture, the means and equipment used in its distribution and the methods of processing data on the basis of which the whole enterprise will be controlled. All this will involve continuous investment in research and resources, and money will have to be found for this investment. Further investment will be required to convince the world that the new inventions are needed and desirable. The whole process will, accordingly, give further emphasis to the fact that financial management is largely a question of appraising and controlling a series of investments.

In order to make a tentative examination of the changes likely to affect business, they may be summarized under the following headings (although there may be various possible viewpoints):

1. A considerable increase in investment by business, covering both physical resources and projects of development, of which an important feature will be the lengthening period before a return can be expected.

2. A continued tendency towards larger groups of corporations, integrated vertically, horizontally, or merely as a form of diversification.
3. Further widening of markets, especially overseas, but also as a result of the demand for increasingly sophisticated products at home.
4. No slackening in the rate of technological advance, particularly in the field of automation (involving feedback devices) and new materials.
5. Further changes in the structure of society, in human attitudes and demands, resulting in part from the widening of education and a parallel reaction against remote government and uniformity.
6. Increased intervention by government in private enterprise in an attempt to reconcile the interests of the State with the interests of the individual and the industrial company.

It will be appreciated that the items are interacting, so that the consequences on the financial control of business can rarely be ascribed to one particular cause. The following sections attempt the bold course of predicting some of the consequences, more to stimulate thought about them than to assume prophetic powers.

1 Increasing investment

From the point of view of the industrial company the term *investment* means, in the present context, the acquisition of resources designed to produce a return some years hence. The areas in which increased investment will be necessary include: automation and computerized data-processing systems, technical, operational, and market research (including economic forecasting), product development, the acquisition of new industrial premises and the adaptation of the old to modern needs, the acquisition and replacement of plant and machinery (the process being accelerated by higher working speeds and growing obsolescence), and training and staff development to meet the needs of the foregoing changes.

The effect of developments of the nature outlined above are likely to change the emphasis of financial planning and control in two major directions. In the first place, because investment is essentially looking to income in the far future, a greater proportion of the effort of financial management must be applied to the methodical appraisal of alternative plans, both from the corporate angle and in regard to individual projects. Because the outgoings made in producing the income, when it eventually emerges, will have been incurred largely in the past, the preoccupation of managers and accountants with current costs will tend to be abortive. The investment made in research, training or the acquisition of specialized plant cannot be reduced after it has been spent; the effort must be directed to making the investment productive.

Investment of the kind described involves special elements of risk. In particular there is the risk that unpredictable external events may contract or eliminate the market to which the investment was directed; changes in technology may make equipment obsolescent or even obsolete before its planned term of usefulness has expired; some of the investment in training is bound to be wasted because a varying percentage of the trainees will leave the company; and a substantial part of advertising and research expenditure is notoriously abortive. Thus, the increased element of risk in business affairs will need correspondingly increased attention by the financial planners. In addition to the normal devices of insurance, forward contracts and hedging, business will make increasing use of leasing and plant hiring contracts. From a wider viewpoint, the association and amalgamation of companies with counter-balancing interests is likely to proceed. Perhaps the most important development may be a significant movement towards self-insurance, through the retention of profits to cover contingencies and possible losses.

The second area in which the changing emphasis towards investment may well have its effect on industrial finances concerns the sourcing and form of the funds obtained for the purpose. It is pertinent to recall that there is little evidence of loyalty or sentiment by investors, institutional or otherwise, towards the companies in which they own shares or debentures. The investor's interest is almost wholly financial; he is concerned with questions of dividend, yield, and growth of capital. Furthermore, successive governments have taken quite positive measures to limit the investor's return from unearned income, by the use of income tax, capital taxes and specific controls. The third factor is that, by using the highly developed facilities of the money market, the investor can and does transfer his interest from one company to another when it suits him to do so.

Thus, except for the smaller company, there exists a widening separation between management and those who supply funds to business, amounting in many cases to an absolute divorce. The interest of management is to obtain finance as cheaply as possible and to maintain a flexible ebb and flow of money according to the varying needs of its investment policy (i.e. investment in resources). The investor's opposing interest is to obtain a high return and to retain freedom of movement for his funds. It therefore seems to us that these contrary interests can be reconciled in the long run only on a contractual basis. The concept of the investor, as a shareholder, owning a slice of the entire undertaking has become outdated and may well be replaced by a contract of loan or deposit giving expressed rights of interest and repayment of capital. It is possible that the interest may move in relation to bank rate.

Building societies operate on lines somewhat similar to those suggested above and some finance companies have obtained the major part of their funds from deposits. Corporation tax has caused a significant rise in debenture issues.

Changes in the form and nature of industrial finance, on the lines indicated, would increase the gearing of companies: it would impose on the management the necessity to meet a high volume of fixed interest on an annual or half-yearly basis, whatever the fortunes of the business in that period. It would also necessitate precise planning for the repayment or conversion of the funds at the due dates. These factors would in turn demand much greater precision in financial planning and control, particularly of internal investment policy. It is also possible that the long-debated argument as to whether interest on capital is a proper ingredient of cost would be settled in the affirmative, thus improving the reality of pricing systems and the consideration of alternative projects.

2 The trend towards larger business groupings

The takeover struggles of post-war years have excited such dramatic interest that less attention has been given to the merits of the amalgamations than to the strategies involved. The ostensible justification for many of the takeovers has been that they produce the advantages of large-scale enterprise in world markets where large-scale businesses based on other countries are operating. More specifically the amalgamations appear to have been designed in many cases to reduce competition by home-based companies, and whilst this may involve the rationalization of the sourcing of supplies, production, and distribution outlets, it has also caused redundancy in men and equipment. Whatever may have been the motivation behind the amalgamations of recent years, we suggest that the prime reason why this trend must continue is to bring into international markets resources, financial and otherwise, comparable with those of foreign competitors.

It is interesting to observe that in some of the less publicized takeovers the purpose has apparently been to achieve what is often a quite widespread diversification of the product line, rather than concentration on traditional lines. In many such cases, the motivation may well have been the need for profitable investment of surplus funds, but the benefits of diversification must also have had considerable influence. As already mentioned, diversification is one means of minimizing risk which, we have suggested, is likely to grow rather than diminish, and we conclude that the future will see an increasing number of large groups with highly diversified interests.

The foregoing refers to the trend towards large groups in the purely private sector of the economy for essentially commercial motives – to maintain a reasonable level of profitability in the long term: for survival. There is also an apparent need to secure the survival of particular industries for national interests, particularly to prevent widespread unemployment; this need again arises largely because of the effect of international competition. This is evident from government intervention, especially in the form of finance, in the computer industry, the aerospace industry and vehicle production, amongst others. Whether this intervention will take the form of complete nationalization or some kind of partnership with private industry – including, perhaps, employees – is an open question; whatever form this governmental interest takes, the resulting organization tends to become enormous, as in those industries mentioned above, as also in coal mining, oil and steel.

Legislation relating to monopolies appears at first sight to be working contrary to the trend, except so far as nationalization is concerned. It is doubtful if in fact this legislation will arrest the formation of large groups; all it is likely to do in face of the pressure of international competition is to ensure that the monopolies act in the national interest. The Monopolies Commission has approved certain monopolies on these grounds. Presumably, the major objection to monopolies is that they may result in excessive profit and high prices, but if, as is likely, industry is financed by fixed interest capital, the incentive to make large profits *for shareholders* is eliminated.

There is little evidence that the large-scale producer operates at lower costs than the smaller concern; the crucial factor is to achieve an optimum size for the producing unit so that it can work on sufficiently long runs and at the same time retain its flexibility and be amenable to direct control of managers who have the power to make decisions. The great enterprise operating on a narrow front may well be a dear producer because of the expense of maintaining intricate systems of checks and controls. The real justification for size is strength of resources, largely financial, which can be applied to investment in modern equipment, the long-term development of products, and the exploitation of markets. For this reason, the large-scale combines of the future may well be of a reasonably diversified structure. For such groupings there would be less danger from government action to prevent the creation of new monopolies.

The financial control of a large, diversified group of companies creates special problems occasioned by the variety of operations to be measured and recorded, the remoteness of centralized management from the operating areas and the difficulty of correctly apportioning expenses amongst the several activities. As already suggested, increased investment in long-term facilities makes the concept of a product cost no longer tenable; the creation of a large, diversified group of enterprises with centralized services can make the allocation of cost to branches, divisions, and departments equally unreal.

The remedy to the problems indicated above lies in the organization of the whole enterprise into self-governing divisions or subsidiaries each of manageable size; this solution has in fact been adopted by many existing groups. It is important that each of these divisions should operate as an independent business, subject only to directives as to group policy, and should maintain its own complete establishment of essential services. Thus, there will be no need for any arbitrary apportionment of the cost of headquarters services, and the major financial function of group management will be to allocate finance where it is likely to be most economically employed. The divisions will be required, as a matter of course, to pay an economic rate of interest on this finance. What is an optimum size for each division is likely to emerge from experience rather than from the application of any theoretical concepts.

The fate of the smaller concern is that it is likely to be embraced by one of the large diversified groups but it will not necessarily lose its individuality or its capacity to provide a personalized service. Alternatively, a number of smaller concerns with similar interests, such as those with affinities of locality or product, may coalesce naturally into a group in order to counter the power of existing groups. Those who resist this process, or have insufficient potential to be absorbed in this way, will inevitably go to the wall because of their inability to sustain the investment required for survival in the competitive world. The really small business, such as the privately owned store, garage, or workshop, may survive for a time by entering into looser associations with similar enterprises. This would entail cooperation in the pooling of finance to meet development and encounter competition; cooperative buying to secure larger discounts; and possibly cooperative publicity, transport, and other services. In any event such looser associations are likely to be more suited to professional and quasi-professional businesses.

3 Widening markets

The natural human need for continual improvement, variety, and change for its own sake indicates that the home market will continue to expand, but it has become clear that British industry must look to the enormous potential of overseas markets to maintain the volume of turnover which is a competitive necessity in many products. Whatever the national interests involved exhortation alone is unlikely to be a decisive factor in inducing a company to undertake the perilous adventure of development overseas. The decisive question for an individual company is whether a better return on capital will be achieved as a result of cultivating overseas markets than by concentration on home sales.

For export sales, the margins are usually small and the effort is invariably great. Once again it is the long view that must be taken – which appears to be the attitude adopted by many companies with substantial overseas interests. The decisive factor is the financial strength which international groups based in foreign countries can apply to the exploitation of a market, largely because of the investment which is required to provide the necessary resources and to endure periods of loss. This strength must be countered not only in export fields but also at home. The accumulation of financial resources to the extent required demands a high volume of interest payments, which in turn will depend on a high volume of sales, and it is unlikely that the required volume will be derived from home markets alone. With narrower profit margins, due to competition and government control, there is little chance of servicing a heavy capitalization from high percentage profits on a limited turnover.

A further circumstance which is likely to accelerate the trend towards larger-scale enterprises is the establishment of international trading communities, such as the Common Market. One result of this circumstance may well be that the inevitable 'shake-out' of the inefficient company will occur not only in relation to its competitors in a particular country, but in relation to its competitors in an international trading community. Subject to this development the further internationalization of trade may be envisaged, and an increase in the establishment of foreign-owned subsidiaries in the various trading countries of the world. These subsidiaries will tend to concentrate on exploiting the specialisms of the parent company, whether those specialisms be derived from natural resources, managerial skill or technological expertise.

The extension of a company's activities to overseas markets gives rise to a fresh set of financial problems of which the confines of this book allow only a very brief indication. The first financial requisite for such a development is to ensure that the information service (which will be largely of an accounting nature) properly segregates the profit, income, costs and other relevant data from the home activities. The most realistic way to accomplish this essential requirement for planning and control is to concentrate all the relevant marketing, administration, and other functions into a separate division or subsidiary company. Such a division, which should be marketing orientated, would probably buy its products at an agreed standard cost, plus interest on capital, from the production department, until a manufacturing organization was set up overseas.

Even where a manufacturing and marketing organization is established overseas, there will remain a need for a policy-making and controlling group to be situated in the domicile of the parent company or, where it is expedient for financial reasons, in a centralized area of overseas operations. This controlling group may be incorporated as a holding company, its main responsibilities being the allocation of finance according to the policy of the group, and its income consisting of interest on the finance which it provides for the subsidiaries. In a number of cases where this kind of structure has been established, a proportion of the finance is raised in overseas money markets.

Apart from the considerable technical expertise and experience necessary for the day-to-day operation of such a development, the initial exercise in forward planning on a long-term basis will need to be supported by continuous replanning in relation to the changes which will inevitably occur in the economic and political structure of each country concerned. Since the objective is essentially financial, the planning, policy making, and control exercises will need a rigorous financial basis.

The planning and administrative problems of overseas

development would impose an impossible burden on the smaller business, but many small businesses, producing specialized products or services, will eventually face the competition of the giants in their home affairs and will be in danger of elimination if they are inefficient, or of being taken over by the large group if they have potential value or constitute a threat. It is possible that, in an interim phase, many of the smaller companies may associate to establish pooled services to deal with export business; but this, we think, must in the long run be the precursor to the formation of a corporate entity of a number of small businesses.

4 Technological developments

The accelerating pace of technology is too apparent to need comment or explanation. It may be said to take the form, so far as industry is concerned, of the production of new materials, improved plant, more scientific processes and systems, and new products. Overshadowing this complex situation is the development of automation which promises to enforce some profound changes in the techniques of financial planning and financial control systems.

Because of the virtual impossibility of quantifying the benefits likely to be derived from pure research (i.e. research without a definite end product in mind), it may be supposed that this activity will tend towards government organizations, endowed or subsidized bodies, such as universities, and those set up by a segment of industry, and possibly the very large groups of companies. In this way, it is foreseeable that the benefits of pure research may be made more widely available, so that the industrial unit can concentrate on perfecting the operations of product development, making, and selling – thus, indeed, intensifying competition in these functions.

With an enhanced flow of new plant, systems, and materials available to industry so will an increased burden be laid on the financial planning operation. The life of a product, and hence of the processes by means of which it was produced, will tend to shorten. In consequence, setting-up costs, and in some cases the cost of specialized machinery and equipment, will need to be recovered in a shorter time than hitherto, while price competition will demand an offsetting rise in the rate of turnover. Increased reliance on market research may be one way of ensuring reasonably accurate forecasting of the sale of new or modified products, but market research is normally an expensive exercise and will add further to the mounting volume of expenses which are of an overhead nature and cannot be directly associated with a unit of production.

Of at least equal significance is the effect of technology applied to the means of production as distinct from the product. New methods and new devices are continually being announced for the purpose either of accelerating production processes or of raising the quality of machining and other operations. Continued developments on these lines will expand the capacity of producing units and thus create pressures to market the greater volume of production. Unless demand can be enlarged to absorb the increased output, financial problems of idle capacity and overstocking will arise. The interplay of supply and demand thus arising will tend to produce changes in price levels, but at the same time the unit cost which has hitherto been used as a basis for pricing policy will have undertaken a radical change.

Where automation and the extension of systems and procedures increase the proportion of indirect costs, until direct costs are practically insignificant, the product cost will become an abstraction without any pretence of reality, resulting from an intricate process of allocation and apportionment. The resulting figure would need adjustment from time to time as the new technology increases the capacity of the workshop. As a basis for pricing, or for considering the profitability of a product, the product cost would be completely disregarded on the grounds that it becomes an unstable and unreal quantity. The science of costing will move more towards the measurement of the efficiency of processes and operations in relation to a time factor. Costing used for the valuation of work in progress will become simply an amount of unrecovered expense, subject to any necessary provisions to reduce it to estimated realizable value, after deducting costs to come. The valuation of finished products may be based on realizable values rather than the purely notional figure of product cost.

The trend towards automation will enforce much more positive and at the same time more flexible long-term planning because of the large expenditure involved in the first place, and of the need to maintain near-capacity working in order to recover that expenditure over a reasonable period of time, in the second place. Once an automated plant is established, the greater part of the costs of production will be of a fixed or period nature and to that extent not amenable to reduction or increase in relation to changing demand. The financial control mechanisms will accordingly have to be directed to ensure that demand is maintained. Forward planning will lean increasingly on the results of market research, probably on a continuing rather than a 'once off' basis. It is probable that the profitability of an automated plant will be incapable of accurate measurement in the traditional calendar year and that the more informative accounts will cover, say, five years of working under a given plan. Since the technology of automation and particularly of its integral element, the computer, will continue to develop and, because of the parallel changes which are likely to take place in the nature of society, political groupings, and markets, the installation of automatic processes and feedback devices in a factory will need modification and perhaps complete reorganization after a period of years. Apart, therefore, from detailed adjustments to the plan from year to year, a major exercise in replanning will need to be undertaken periodically, say once every five years. Such replanning is likely to involve further injections of capital which it will be logical to obtain, so far as possible, from internal resources to cover replacement of machinery and equipment and the reorientation of administrative services.

The automatic factory is already in existence and the signs indicate that it will eventually become commonplace. Before this occurs profound changes are likely in the nature of industrial management and in the skills required of the subordinate worker. The latter involves retraining the craftsman so that he is converted into either a technician (with changed skills) or a planner.

Much will no doubt be done under government auspices; but a substantial element of the retraining will take place within the companies involved in the new technology as a more direct means of ensuring that they command the services of the skilled employees without which automation cannot proceed.

In addition to the effort and expense of retraining the older employee in new skills, business must become increasingly involved in the development *ab initio* of the younger employee towards the new technologies. There is a growing need for the academic world to prepare its students for the age of automation and, because academia adapts slowly to change, the necessary courses in the field of further and higher education may have to be largely subsidized by business; business may have to exert a more direct interest in the courses offered by the academic institutions concerned.

An incidental but important aspect of the new technology is that, even with extensive training and retraining, many employees who are unable to adapt to the new skills required will become redundant; and many younger people may be unsuited to the new work environment and become unemployable. If such a situation is not overcome humanely and efficiently, industrial conflict will result, which for business means unproductive effort, loss of turnover and reduced profits. Some of the more obvious remedies are shorter hours, early retirement and improved pension schemes. For a particular business both the situation and the remedies involve administrative effort and cost – a cost not attributable to the making or selling of goods and services.

The rapid development in industrial technology, then, will bring increased administrative burdens and higher overheads to business generally. This prediction enforces the need for careful financial planning of a long-term nature. The major remedies should lie with the effects of increasing efficiency and automated processes; for those factors should bring in their train increases in turnover which, with adequate planning and control, should provide sufficient surplus to pay for the additional expenditure.

5 Changes in society

Business operates within the boundaries of a highly organized society and must be prepared to conform to its rules and conventions. The changes which are occurring in the structure of society, and in the nature of human needs and desires, are a necessary subject of study for managers. This book is not an appropriate medium for the examination of these complex changes, nor are the authors competent to do this. But it is proper to draw attention to some of the broader movements in the nature of society which are relevant to business and its financial management.

So far as the employment of people is concerned, the present situation in this and most industrialized nations is that demand for skilled labour exceeds supply. It has been suggested that this situation may be reversed by the development of automation, but even if this becomes true in general terms, automation is likely to create a more intensive shortage of the specialized skills which *it* demands. It is reasonable to suppose that it is the excess of demand for skilled employees over supply which has enhanced the independence of the employee, particularly when he is organized or organizes himself in large or small groups. This independence leads to a questioning attitude by employees towards management decisions which affect the interests of the former. The working force is no longer prepared to accept submissively such features of industrial life as managerial intolerance, inequalities of pay or redundancy. The widespread feeling that the rights of the individual must be enforced against a faceless bureaucracy is particularly prevalent amongst the younger members of the community, from whose ranks the managers of the future will be recruited. There will be a growing acceptance of the idea that the work force of a company will need to be consulted, through its elected representatives, when major questions of objectives and policy arise.

These conclusions will be emphasized by the declining power of the investor to influence the operations of an industrial group of large size. In *The Liberal Hour* J. K. Galbraith maintains that: 'The power lies with the professional manager ... they select the board of directors, which the stockholders then dutifully elect, and in equally solemn ritual the board then selects the management that elected it.' If this is in fact the case then it will be the subordinate employees who, together with the state, exercise a controlling influence over the managers.

In what manner will the increasing influence of a company's employees affect financial management? If questions of cost, price, profit and capital continue to be the key factors in business, then the interests of the employees can affect all kinds of managerial decisions. The influence of the subordinate employees is unlikely to extend to the day-to-day administration of the business, nor necessarily will the employees enforce a greater share out of income, because intensive competition will not permit excessive remuneration for any factor of production. The influence of the employees will be most significantly seen in the manner in which appropriations of profit will be made.

The first charge against after-tax profits will clearly be the contractual rate of interest on the capital (which is likely to be largely in the form of loans or deposits). The second charge will be transfers to reserves for the purpose of maintaining capital intact, in the face of changing money values, obsolescence, and the need to provide for asset replacement and applied research. Subject to such residue of equity capital as may remain, the balance of the profit may be considered available for what may be termed 'policy appropriations'. It is in the disposal of this balance that the employees' influence will probably be felt.

Policy appropriations might be taken to mean appropriations for the maintenance of goodwill; in this context goodwill will need to be maintained in two specific directions – the goodwill of the market and the goodwill of the labour force. In the first it is conceivable that surplus profits may be applied to the reduction of the price of the products, the improvement of quality and the provision of an enhanced service. In the second direction the appropriations may well consist of the improvement of employee amenities; more in the area of provisions for education, training and retraining, security, retirement, and aid in sickness and other calamities, than in social activities or individual monetary awards. No doubt there would be a tug of war between these two aspects of goodwill, but conflict is not unusual in business.

The foregoing does nothing to detract from the influence of the profit motive. If such forecasts come about, the profit motive will become a more powerful influence than ever before in stimulating efficiency, and may even become respectable. If it is felt that these predictions are fanciful, they are already in the minds of many sections of top-level management and are influencing, even now, decisions by boards of directors, in approving policy and appropriations.

There is no place in this book for speculation on the eventual form which the much discussed 'industrial democracy' will take; it is relevant to mention effects which that movement may have on financial planning. Two aspects of industrial democracy which are already in existence are the appointment of worker directors, especially in nationalized undertakings, and the establishment of worker cooperatives in the shipbuilding and motorcycle manufacturing industries. There are other and older examples of worker cooperatives associated with private enterprise. There is no essential difference so far as the objectives of financial planning are concerned between these organizations and any other form of private enterprise. In all cases there is a need to plan and obtain a surplus sufficient to retain capital and attract additional capital; likewise a need for finance to enable the organization to pay its debts.

6 Government intervention in industry

The future course of government intervention in industry is difficult to predict because such trends as are evident have been overlaid and sophisticated by political and ideological argument and pressures. But if the events of recent years are any guide, it *is* possible to predict with some confidence that government intervention will increase rather than diminish. Perhaps the outstanding reason for the government exercising positive means of regulating industry is the fact that the country has become, in the face of intense international competition, a trading unit in itself. The association with the Common Market will accelerate the process because of the need for the state to intervene to ensure conformity with the decrees of the community.

The government thus has an increasing responsibility for the financial and economic regulation of the country and this must involve restrictions on the actions, both of the supplier of goods and services and of the consumer: the intervention must affect the manufacturer as well as his markets. There will presumably be a continuing responsibility for defence which is likely to confirm the government as the great buyer of goods and services from industry. Defence needs involve continuous technological research, which may well become more concentrated in government hands, but which also makes use of industrial services. The conclusions of such research frequently have important industrial applications.

There are ample signs that the needs of the nation for welfare facilities will develop rather than lessen, and whilst these services may continue to be organized and administered largely by government departments, it is reasonable to suppose that the increased cost will have to be borne by industry as well as by the individual. As mentioned above, the national need for improvements in industrial training and retraining is likely to receive further emphasis by the development of automation. The effort involved, if not the cost, must continue to be borne largely by industry because the training must be essentially vocational if it is to be relevant to national needs. To the extent that this process of further education can be conducted in the classroom, industrial companies may well feel a continuing duty to provide financial aid to local and even national academic institutions.

The following is an attempt to summarize broadly the nature of the changes which are likely to emerge from the trends outlined above:

(a) DIRECT INTERVENTION

This heading would include an intensification of governmental powers to intervene in monopolies, interest rates, credit control, import, export and currency regulations, and possibly the supply of capital.

(b) GOVERNMENT REPRESENTATION

The government may well extend its power and ability to take a direct financial interest in selected groups of industrial concerns, in order to encourage development which is considered to be in the national interest. For this reason, and because the community will consider it desirable for the government to have a closer watching brief over the day-to-day decisions of a powerful industrial group, there will be increasing state representation on the boards of many such groups. It is probable that a government representative on a board will find himself holding the balance between any conflicting interests which may arise between the employee members and the professional managers. It is likely that he will endeavour to enforce adherence to the concept of the 'fair price' and the 'fair return' on investment. Those concepts, which are now decidedly nebulous in character, may eventually be given some precision through the evolution of commonly accepted rules and conventions.

(c) FINANCIAL MEASURES

Financial measures, largely in the form of taxation and credit control, are likely to remain variable according to the changing needs of the economy. It must be hoped that such measures become more rationalized and therefore more predictable. There may be more universal acceptance of taxation as an element of cost, along with interest on capital, and thus it may influence more scientific pricing policies. The benefit of treating taxation and interest as costs is that such a process may cause more logical differentials in prices, rather than all-round increases.

Many of the detailed financial effects on a business of government intervention are implicit in the nature of that intervention. In general terms government actions in relation to industry will produce two broad effects: (a) the financial responsibilities of management will widen beyond the need to satisfy investors' interests and (b) measures will be taken by management to overcome the worst effects of the variability of government policies, particularly in the financial field.

Because of the lessening influence of the shareholder, and the increasing influence of the state and the employees as a body, the large group will tend to bend its policies more towards satisfying national and social needs. These needs may well be exemplified in the form of the fair price, concentration on export, cost benefit analysis, community needs, protection of the employees, and training. The growth and stability of the group will, no doubt, remain the overriding consideration of management, but a policy of accepting the responsibilities indicated above may be pursued if only as a means of ensuring group prosperity.

The problem of coping with variable government policies and practices, especially in the field of financial regulators, will create a movement for industry to become independent of these regulators. This implies the building up of sufficient financial strength and flexibility to weather the recessions and changes of course in taxation, import and export controls, and credit and exchange restrictions, to name the more obvious of the weapons available to the government. The means by which such strength and flexibility could be attained are really the essential skills of good management, but they would certainly involve a large measure of self-financing, by adequate retentions, diversification and other devices of self-insurance, and the maintenance of liquidity. All these means are available to the large combination, but few to the small independent business, unless it enters into arrangements with others for pooling resources.

The growth of government purchasing activities seems inevitable, but the principles and practices used in the pricing of government contracts is a matter of controversy and, indeed, emotion. Once again, the concept of the fair price and the fair return on capital are supposed to be applied, but as yet no one seems to have found a way of quantifying risk, which is inherent in these concepts. It is doubtful whether the principle of equal disclosure of information will ever work satisfactorily in the field of business which contains most of the elements of a continuing battle. Without solutions to these problems government departments may well either (a) be forced to enter into commercial markets on the same basis as other buyers or (b) provide more of the goods and services they need from their own resources. Business with large interests in goverment work cannot continue to operate indefinitely under the threat of post audits, or without sufficient surpluses to create reserves which will offset the increasing risks of large-scale and long-term projects.

The above should be viewed as a tentative but honest attempt to grapple with some of the enormous and complex problems of the future. The themes are: the inevitable trend towards large groupings of enterprise; a further decline in the shareholders' effectiveness; an increase in government intervention; a re-shaping of industrial objectives; the overriding need for planning on a long-term basis. Some or many of this book's predictions may be proved wrong; certainly many of its conclusions, whether right or wrong, will cause gloom and despondency, annoyance, and even scorn. What is being asked of the reader is that he consider the facts, interpret the trends and prepare for the future. This, too, is management.

Further reading

Finance and Accounts for Managers by Desmond Goch, Pan Books; specially written for non-accounting managers; sets out the essentials of finance and accounting.

Financial and Cost Accounting for Management by Taylor and Shearing; Macdonald and Evans; also written for the non-accounting manager; explains the technicalities of accounting and costing in adequate depth.

Standard Costing by Batty; Macdonald and Evans; a thoroughgoing exposition of standard costing techniques.

Managerial Accounting by Rossell and Frasure; C. E. Merrill; an extensive treatment.

Management of Company Finance by Samuels and Wilkes; Nelson; extensive, somewhat advanced treatment of the purely financial aspects of business.

The Capital Budgeting Decision by Bierman and Smidt; Macmillan, New York; a standard and well written text on the subject.

Fieldhouse's Income Tax Simplified by Arthur Fieldhouse; Fieldhouse; essentials of UK taxation.

Budgeting: Profit Planning and Control by Glenn Welsch; Prentice Hall; a book for managers; a good conceptual basis and practical applications.

Cost Accounting: a Managerial Emphasis by Horngren; Prentice Hall; comprehensive textbook on costing, budgeting and financial planning; useful for reference.

Index

Desmond Goch

Finance and Accounts for Managers £1.25

The art of accountancy is now the most important instrument of control in the management armoury. This comprehensive guide will enable managers – even those without formal training in business finance – to formulate trading policies, forecast future trends and effectively administer their departments.

Rosemary Stewart

The Reality of Management £1.25

'Not just another manual for executives, it is rather more like a set of compass bearings to help the manager plot his course in his career and his social life' NEW SOCIETY

The Reality of Organizations £1.25

'Addressed to managers whether in industry, commerce, hospitals, public administration or elsewhere and includes examples from these latter fields . . . its style is excellent, concise and free of jargon' PUBLIC ADMINISTRATION